FAITH IN THE MAKING

90 Days of Grace While Becoming.

By Tandra Wade

© 2026 Tandra Wade
All rights reserved.

Published by **Apex Pillars Group LLC**

No part of this book may be reproduced, distributed, stored in a retrieval system, or transmitted in any form or by any means electronic, mechanical, photocopying, recording, or otherwise without prior written permission from the publisher, except for brief quotations in reviews and certain other noncommercial uses permitted by copyright law.

Scripture quotations marked **NIV** are taken from **The Holy Bible, New International Version® (NIV®)**.
Copyright © 1973, 1978, 1984, 2011 by Biblica, Inc.® Used by permission. All rights reserved worldwide.

This book is based on personal experiences and reflections. Names, identifying details, and certain circumstances may have been changed to protect privacy.

ISBN: 979-8-9947104-0-1

Printed in the United States of America.

This book is dedicated to my son. My greatest teacher, my biggest why, and the reason I learned how to keep going even when I was tired.

To my mother for showing me what strength looks like in real life and for covering me in ways I didn't understand until I became a woman.

And to every woman still trying, still healing, still hoping, still believing, still becoming… this is for you.

May these pages feel like a deep breath, a mirror, and a reminder that God hasn't let you go.

"You were taught, with regard to your former way of life, to put off your old self, which is being corrupted by its deceitful desires; to be made new in the attitude of your minds; and to put on the new self, created to be like God in true righteousness and holiness."

— Ephesians 4: 22-24

TABLE OF CONTENTS
SECTION 1 — WE WAS OUTSIDE

Day 1. Nine In A Neon 2
Day 2. Lucky Girl Syndrome 5
Day 3. Check The Mail 8
Day 4. The Green Water Pool 11
Day 5. That's Corny 13
Day 6. Snow Days 15
Day 7. Ringing The Bell 17
Day 8. The Fun House 19
Day 9. The Happy Meal Job 21
Day 10. Back In My Day 23

SECTION 2 — THE STORIES THAT RAISED ME

Day 11. Laughing So I Don't Cry 26
Day 12. The House That Never Slept 30
Day 13. The Shoes That Taught Me Perspective 32
Day 14. When Adults Forget To Lead 34
Day 15. Loyalty At All Cost 36
Day 16. What Water Couldn't Wash Away 38
Day 17. Left In The Middle 40
Day 18. The Day I Didn't Go 42
Day 19. When Nothing Registered 44
Day 20. The Face Of Grief 46

SECTION 3 — MAMA MODE

Day 21. Carrying Him Alone 49
Day 22. For Such A Time As This 52

Day 23. Selfless Parenting 54
Day 24. Trying To Make Up The Hours 56
Day 25. Looking Like I Had It Together 58
Day 26. When His Struggles Feel Like Failure 60
Day 27. Let Them Be Little 62
Day 28. Meeting Them Where They Are 65
Day 29. Choosing Blessed Over Worried 68
Day 30. The Healing Drive 71

SECTION 4 — LOVE LESSONS (WHEW)

Day 31. She Does It Anyway 75
Day 32. What Looked Like A Blessing 78
Day 33. Afraid To Let Go 81
Day 34. When Everything Was Taken 84
Day 35. Watching From The Outside 87
Day 36. Learning How To Receive Love 89
Day 37. Love, Lust, Foundation 92
Day 38. Guard Your Ear, Protect Your Peace 95
Day 39. When Love Remains But Alignment Changes 98
Day 40. Don't Look Back 101

SECTION 5 — GOD IN THE DETAILS

Day 41. Miracles All Around 106
Day 42. When You Don't Have To Prove It 109
Day 43. When I Let The Internet Tell Me I Needed More 112
Day 44. When The Enemy Makes You Question Your Identity
.... 114
Day 45. The Version God Sees 117
Day 46. God's Favorite 121

Day 47. Fresh Start 125
Day 48. Knowing When To Ask For Help 129
Day 49. There's No Wrong Way To Pray 132
Day 50. Choosing Grace Over Crashing Out 135

SECTION 6 — HARD LESSONS, SOFT HEART

Day 51. A Hard Head Makes A Soft Butt 140
Day 52. Trusting God In The Simple Seasons 142
Day 53. Faith That Keeps Me Afloat 145
Day 54. Fasting With Intention 150
Day 55. Online, But Still All In 153
Day 56. Power Of The Tongue 157
Day 57. Alignment Vs. Opportunity 159
Day 58. Delusional Faith 162
Day 59. Uniquely Positioned 166
Day 60. Dark Enough To Hear 169

SECTION 7 — SOFT LIFE, STRONG SPIRIT

Day 61. Soft Life, Strong Spirit 172
Day 62. Hakuna Matata 177
Day 63. Expectations 181
Day 64. Successful, But Still Searching 184
Day 65. The Smallest In The Room 186
Day 66. Someone Else's Dream 189
Day 67. When Hard Work Isn't Enough 192
Day 68. When Faith Requires A Leap 195

Day 69. God Met Me Where I Was 198
Day 70. Choosing Conviction Over Comfort 201

SECTION 8 — THE PIVOT SEASON

Day 71. Outgrown Environments 205
Day 72. Finding My Way 208
Day 73. When Perspective Walks Past You 211
Day 74. Perfection Obsession 214
Day 75. Rejection Recharge 217
Day 76. Oh, I Wanna Move Here 220
Day 77. Rich, Blessed, Still Hungry 223
Day 78. New Car Faith 227
Day 79. You Think You All That 231
Day 80. World Ready Vs. Word Ready 234

SECTION 9 — FINISH STRONG

Day 81. Clean That Car 239
Day 82. Birthdays Behind Bars 243
Day 83. Sarah 247
Day 84. Seeing The Person Not The Prison 251
Day 85. Cancer Who? 255
Day 86. Logging Out To Tune In 259
Day 87. I Can't Fail 262
Day 88. Side Quest 265
Day 89. The First Time I Bet On Myself 269
Day 90. This Is The Day 273

PREFACE

I didn't set out to write a "perfect" devotional.

I wrote this because I kept hearing the same thing, in different ways, from friends, family, and women who look like they've got it together but are still carrying a lot underneath: "I'm trying."

Trying to heal.

Trying to forgive.

Trying to let go.

Trying to trust God when life doesn't make sense.

Trying to become someone new without feeling like you have to erase who you've been.

This book was born in a season of transition. The kind where you realize stability doesn't always mean peace, growth isn't always pretty, and every experience connects to the next. As I started reflecting on the stories I lived through: childhood memories, grief, motherhood, relationships, work, identity, disappointment, and the quiet wins nobody claps for, a realization emerged: God was in all of it.

He was present not just in the breakthroughs, but right in the middle when things felt uncertain.

In the messy.

Even in the "I don't know what I'm doing, but I'm still here" moments, His presence remained consistent.

Faith in the Making: 90 Days of Grace While Becoming is a daily journey built on real life and the real Word. Each day includes a scripture (NIV), a story, reflection questions, and a prayer not just for reading, but to help you feel seen, held, and guided. The journey weaves laughter, honest reflection, and moments of relief. Most importantly, everyday points you back to God and reminds you that you're not behind. To help you put faith into action, try setting aside time each day to reflect on the reading and its message: journaling, discussing with a friend, or meditating can help integrate these lessons into life's ups and downs.

If you miss a day, don't quit or restart out of shame. Just keep going, grace is part of the process.

This devotional is for the woman who's still becoming.

Still learning.

Still healing.

Still choosing God even when she's tired.

And if that's you, welcome.

Let's grow!

First, all glory to God.

Thank You for keeping me, correcting me, covering me, and continuing to build me even in seasons where I felt stuck, tired, or unsure. Thank You for the grace that held me together when I didn't have the words, and for the purpose You kept pulling out of my life piece by piece.

To my son, thank you for making me better. Thank you for your patience with me, your joy, your honesty, and your love. You're the reason I fight for growth, the reason I choose healing, and the reason I keep showing up. You've taught me more about grace than any book ever could.

To my mother, thank you for being the foundation. For your sacrifices, your strength, your prayers, your laughter, and your love. Thank you for always making a way, always holding the family together, and always reminding me who I am.

To my family and friends, thank you for giving me grace through every version of me. Thank you for the encouragement, the late-night talks, the check-ins, the laughs, the honest feedback, and the moments that reminded me I wasn't doing life alone. Thank you for letting my story be my story and still loving me through it.

To every pastor, mentor, and spiritual voice who poured into me, thank you for teaching the Word in ways that reached my real life. Thank you for helping me grow from believing to becoming.

And to every woman still trying, THANK YOU! Your resilience matters. Your healing matters. Your story matters. If you're still trying, God is still working. I pray these pages remind you that grace isn't the end of the journey, it's the way you make it through.

With love,

Tandra Wade

HOW TO USE THIS DEVOTIONAL

This isn't a book you rush through.

It's a space you return to. Faith in the Making: 90 Days of Grace While Becoming was written for the woman who's growing in real time, the one who's learning, healing, and still showing up even when she doesn't feel "ready."

Here's how to move through this devotional, following its daily structure:

1) You don't have to begin on Day 1. If you're led to a section, start there. Grace covers the journey.

2) Read the scripture first.

Let the Word set the tone before the story sets the mood. Read it slowly. Read it twice if you need to. Sit with it.

3) Read the story like a mirror, not a movie.

Some days will feel light. Some days may hit a tender place. Let it. Healing isn't always loud, but it's always honest.

4) Answer the reflection questions in your own way.

Write a sentence. Write a paragraph. Write one. There is no "right" response, just a real one.

5) Pray the prayer out loud if you can. Even if it's quiet or shaky, or you can't find the words, God hears you. Remember, your spiritual journey doesn't need to be perfect.

6) If you miss a day, simply continue. What matters is your intention and heart, not perfection.

Just keep going. You're not behind. You're becoming.

7) Come back and reread when you need it.

Some devotionals are for the day you read them.

Some are for the day you finally understand them.

Take your time.

Let the stories soften you.

Let the Word anchor you.

Let grace meet you in the middle.

And remember, you can be faithful even if you're still in progress.

SECTION 1: WE <u>WAS</u> OUTSIDE

NINE IN A NEON

This is one of those stories that still makes me laugh every time I think about it.

There was a party on the other side of town, and we had to be there.

If you grew up in the early 2000s, you already know the vibe business casual meets clubwear. We were all dressed up, matching, ready to be seen.

The only problem?

Only one of us had a car.

A Neon.

If you don't know what a Neon is… just picture a tiny little sedan that was not built for nine fully grown teenage girls.

But did that stop us?

Absolutely not.

We piled in.

One friend sat halfway on the center console.

Two were stacked in the passenger seat.

The rest of us were layered in the back like luggage.

When we got to the party, we parked far down the street because we knew getting out was going to be an event. Nobody could even open their own door. The driver had to go around opening each one while we tumbled out headfirst.

We were packed in that car like sardines, but we made it.

And we didn't just show up.

We showed up together.

All matching. Red, black, and white. Pin-up girl outfits. Polka dots. Poofy skirts. Red lipstick. We walked in like a unit.

We didn't have money.

We didn't have rides.

We didn't have convenience.

But we had determination.

I think about that now, and how today, it's easy to wait for convenience. But back then, nothing was easy; we made things happen anyway. We didn't let obstacles keep us from showing up for what mattered to us.

There's something holy about that kind of perseverance, even when it was just about going to a party.

Because when you really want something, you'll make a way.

Scripture

"Blessed is the one who perseveres under trial because, having stood the test, that person will receive the crown of life that the Lord has promised."

— James 1:12

Reflection Questions

- When was the last time I pushed through inconvenience to enjoy something?
- Do I still show up with the same determination I used to?
- Where in my life have I been waiting for things to be easy instead of just moving?

Prayer

God, help me not lose the joy and determination I had when I was younger. Remind me that sometimes the journey is just as beautiful as the destination.

Amen.

LUCKY GIRL SYNDROME
(But make it faith)

When people talk about "lucky girl syndrome," I don't think about magic. I think about momentum. I think about what happens when I start my day on purpose.

Like those mornings when I wake up, and I pray. I turn on my affirmations. I wash my face. I clean my house. I put on some old music because you know you're in a good mood when Anita Baker is playing and it feels like peace is sitting with you.

Then I step out to run errands, and it's the smallest things that start happening.

I go to Target and somehow, I'm gifted a little promotional box they're giving out. I'm like, *dang… thanks.*

Then I hit Aldi's, and if you've ever been, you know you need a quarter for the cart. I don't have one. I'm already thinking that I'm about to carry everything around the store like a goofball, and a person just hands me their cart like it's nothing. *Dang… that was lucky.*

Or I'm running late somewhere, trying to turn into traffic, and nobody's letting me in… then one person stops and waves me through. All green lights the rest of the way. *Dang… that was lucky.*

But the truth is… It's not luck.

It's what happens when I start my day looking for God instead of looking for what's wrong. When I begin with gratitude, I notice grace. When I begin with peace, I move with peace. And peace has a way of attracting more peace.

I've learned that if I focus on what's good, my spirit stays open. My energy stays light. My attitude stays soft. And the day starts lining up differently, not because the world changed, but because *I* did.

And then there's the bigger part of it too: vision.

I'm learning to remember the future the way I remember the past. To see it so clearly that it feels familiar. I can already picture the home I want. I can see me and my partner hosting family nights, football on the big screen, everybody laughing, cards on the table, love in the room. I can see my son leading prayer with confidence because I raised him to know God.

That's not delusion. That's faith with a picture.

Because when God places a vision in you, it's not to tease you, it's to guide you. And when you start your day with gratitude, you start your day with agreement: *"God, I trust You. I believe You. I'm expecting good."*

So, if you want "lucky girl syndrome," start here:
Gratitude. Vision. Alignment.
And watch how grace keeps finding you.

Scripture

"Give thanks in all circumstances; for this is God's will for you in Christ Jesus."

— 1 Thessalonians 5:18

Reflection Questions

- What "small graces" have I overlooked lately?
- How does my morning routine affect my mood and my mindset?
- What future am I asking God for and can I see it clearly?

Prayer

God, thank You for the small blessings I usually rush past. Help me start my days with gratitude and expectation, not anxiety and fear. Align my mind with Your peace and my heart with Your vision. Teach me to notice grace in the little moments and trust You with the bigger ones. In Jesus' name, Amen.

CHECK THE MAIL

It sounds silly, but this story taught me something I'll never forget.

If you've ever lived in an apartment where your mailbox isn't connected to your front door, you know how easy it is to ignore your mail. You don't avoid it because it's not important; you avoid it because most of the time, it's just bad news. Bills. Coupons. Ads. Things asking you for money you don't have.

So I used to let my mail sit. Weeks at a time.

One day, I finally checked it... and inside was one of those scratch-off dealership flyers. You know the ones, "You could win $25,000!"

I scratched it.

And I won.

I was staring at $25,000 on a piece of paper. In that season of my life, that kind of money would've been life changing. I had a child. I was grinding. I could've used every dollar.

But there was a catch.

It had expired.

The dealership was literally five minutes from my house... but the deadline had passed because the flyer had been sitting in my mailbox.

That taught me: sometimes blessings are missed because we don't look, expecting only the usual disappointment.

And that made me think…

How many times in life do we ignore something because we're used to it being bad news?

How many opportunities do we miss because we assume nothing good is coming?

How many blessings are sitting right in front of us… unopened?

Sometimes God sends breakthroughs wrapped in ordinary envelopes.

But if we never check… We'll never know.

Scripture

"Forget the former things; do not dwell on the past. See, I am doing a new thing! Now it springs up; do you not perceive it?"

—Isaiah 43: 18–19

Reflection

- What have you been avoiding because you expect disappointment?
- Is there something God may be trying to show you that you keep overlooking?
- What "mail" do you need to finally open?

Prayer

God, help me not to miss what You're trying to give me. Teach me to stay open, even when I've been disappointed before. Remind me that not every message is bad news, and not every door is closed. Give me the courage to check what you've placed in front of me, even when I'm afraid it won't be good.

In Jesus' name, Amen.

THE GREEN WATER POOL

There was one house in our neighborhood that was considered the nice house.

We started out in the housing projects, then moved down the street to smaller houses, and eventually, we made it to the big house. And that big house was the only one with a pool. To us, that meant we had made it.

The pool was filthy. The lining was torn. Everything about it said it needed professional help and money we didn't have. But my stepdad was determined. Before YouTube tutorials, before TikTok, he decided he was going to fix that pool himself. He shocked it. Drained it. Cleaned it. Worked on it over and over again. And still, the water stayed green.

But that didn't stop him. He tested the water in front of us and told us it was safe. And we believed him. You couldn't tell us nothing; we were getting in that pool. Green water and all. We lived our best lives in that pool. Laughing, swimming, making memories. I even remember telling another kid they couldn't get in because they were mean to me. That was my pool.

Now I laugh thinking about it, half-joking that one day there will be a commercial asking if we swam in a green pool as kids. But underneath the humor is something real. My stepdad didn't give up because the pool wasn't perfect. He didn't stop because it didn't look the way it was supposed to. He kept going because his goal wasn't perfection; it was our happiness.

That pool taught me something early: love doesn't always show up polished. Sometimes it shows up trying. Sometimes it shows up doing the best it can with limited resources. Grace lives in those moments. In an effort. In intention. In showing up even when the outcome isn't flawless.

Scripture

"My grace is sufficient for you, for my power is made perfect in weakness."

— 2 Corinthians 12:9

Reflection Questions

- Where have you experienced love that showed up imperfectly but sincerely?
- How do you define "enough" in your own life today?
- What would it look like to give grace to effort instead of expecting perfection?

Prayer

God, thank You for the people who loved me through effort and intention, not perfection. Help me recognize grace in the trying and remind me that imperfect love still counts.

Amen.

THAT'S CORNY

I can't believe I'm turning into my mom.

I catch myself asking my son to do little things I think are cool, only for him to look at me like I'm corny. And every time it happens, I'm taken right back to my childhood.

My friends and I used to make up dance steps. We burned CDs, made mix tapes, and practiced routines over and over. My house was one of the houses where we practiced, or my friend's house, whose mom was the same kind of supportive. She'd stand in the screen door, watching us repeat the same steps until we got it right. My mom did the same.

When my mom's friends came over, she'd ask me to do the dance even if my friends weren't there. I hated it. I thought it was embarrassing. Corny. Sometimes she'd even try to add her own input: "What if you did this instead?" And I'd be annoyed. "Mom, that's butt."

Now I get it.

As a parent, there's a little ache that comes when your child doesn't want to do the things you're excited about. When your enthusiasm isn't shared. But what I understand now is that when parents ask you to show off, even in the smallest ways, it's not about performance. It's about pride. It's about watching your child do something good and feeling like, maybe I did something right.

Whether it was a dance, a rap, or finishing a Busta Rhymes verse from start to finish, those moments mattered more than I realized. What felt corny to me was joy to her. What felt small to me was everything to her.

Grace teaches us to cherish the moments before they become memories. To honor the love behind the request. And to remember that being seen, especially by the people who raised us, is a gift we don't fully understand until time teaches us how.

Scripture

"Children are a heritage from the Lord."

— Psalm 127:3

Reflection Questions

- What moments from your childhood do you see differently now as an adult?
- How do you show pride in the people you love today?
- What small moments might God be asking you to cherish right now?

Prayer

God, help me see joy the way You do. Teach me to cherish moments as I live them and to honor the love behind the things I once took for granted.

Amen.

SNOW DAYS

It always makes me feel a little old when I say, "back in my day," especially when I'm talking to my son. He's growing up in Georgia, and my childhood in Pittsburgh looks nothing like his. He's navigating things I never had, like social media, constant noise, and pressure that follows you everywhere. And sometimes I find myself trying to explain what we had in place of it.

I remember waking up early on winter mornings, glued to the TV, waiting for Pittsburgh Public Schools to scroll across the bottom of the screen, announcing a closure. When it finally did, there was no staying in the house. My friends and I grabbed our shovels and our wagon and walked to the top of the hill to fill buckets with salt. Then we headed to the nicer neighborhoods. House to house. Fifty houses sometimes. Eight to ten of us, knocking on doors, shoveling snow for money. That was our business.

By the end of the day, we'd make our way to the store, buy food and snacks, and head home tired but proud. We didn't sit around watching TV on snow days; we worked. We learned how to make something out of nothing.

What stands out just as much is how my mom prepared us. She layered us up from head to toe. She put grocery store bags over our socks before we put on our shoes to keep our feet dry. We'd be sweating under all those layers while shoveling walkways for hours. And somehow, every time I came home, my hands would still be frostbitten. She did what she could with what she had.

Looking back, I see how much that shaped me. Work ethic. Resourcefulness. Community. Drive. We didn't call it a hustle; we just called it what you did. Grace met us there, too. In frozen fingers, full days, and the pride of earning something with your hands.

Times have changed, but the foundation remains. And I'm grateful for the way those snow days helped build who I am today.

Scripture

"The one who is unwilling to work shall not eat."

— 2 Thessalonians 3:10

Reflection Questions

- What childhood responsibilities shaped your work ethic?
- How did your parents prepare you with what they had?
- In what ways are you passing those lessons on to the next generation?

Prayer

God, thank You for the lessons hidden in ordinary days. Help me honor where I came from and pass forward the values that shaped me with wisdom and grace.

Amen.

RINGING THE BELL

Before I was even ten years old, I was part of the Salvation Army on my own. It was right up the street in our neighborhood, and for us kids, it was easy to belong. They had a free summer food program, after-school activities, a computer lab upstairs in the library, an open gym, toys, a choir, and a band. That's where I learned how to play the trumpet. It wasn't just a place to pass the time; it was a place that gave us an opportunity.

During the holidays, they would take us kettling. The captain's daughters and I, along with a few other kids, would get dressed in little pea coats, dress slacks, and dress shoes. We'd be dropped off at different spots in the mall and stand outside ringing bells next to those red Salvation Army buckets. I didn't even fully understand what the money was for at the time; it was just my job. And I took it seriously.

It was cold. Freezing actually. But I didn't think about that. What I remember most is the pride I felt. Standing there, ringing that bell, playing my trumpet sometimes, knowing I was doing something that mattered. At the end of the night, they'd crack open the kettles and count how much we raised, and it felt so good to see the impact. We even got paychecks. At such a young age, responsibility and service were being sewn into me without me realizing it.

Now, as an adult, I look back and laugh. I've teased my mom before, asking how she could let us get dropped off at the mall for hours at night in a world like this. But the truth is, we grew up in different times. And what we were doing wasn't reckless. It was meaningful. It taught me humility. It taught me discipline. It taught me that giving, whether it's time, effort, or presence, matters.

I didn't know it then, but God was already shaping my heart for service. Long before I had language for purpose, He was teaching me how to show up.

Scripture

"Don't let anyone look down on you because you are young, but set an example for the believers in speech, in conduct, in love, in faith and in purity."

— 1 Timothy 4:12

Reflection Questions

- Where were you learning responsibility or service before you understood its value?
- What early experiences shaped your sense of pride in doing good?
- How might God have been forming your character long before you recognized Him?

Prayer

God, thank You for the early lessons I didn't fully understand. Thank You for planting seeds of service, humility, and purpose in me before I knew what to call them. Help me honor those foundations and continue to show up with the same heart today.

Amen.

THE FUN HOUSE

Looking back, we weren't rich. But my mom always made a way.

My sister and I were born four years and five days apart, and every year she turned our birthdays into something special. Our basement became the place for sleepovers; the kind people talked about. She'd go to the dollar store and grab prizes, and we'd set up dance competitions. The older girls acted as coaches, helping us choreograph routines. We played hide-and-seek, did fashion shows, and laughed all night. All the things little girls dream of. At the time, it felt normal to me. That was just our house.

I didn't realize how special it was until later. Being invited to our sleepovers was a big deal. One year, I showed up late to my best friend's birthday party, and when I walked in, everyone rushed toward me, her friends, even her mom. Her mom said, "I've been waiting for you to get here. I need you to tell me what to do." She explained that all her daughter talked about was wanting her sleepover to be like ours. She wanted to make it just as good. She needed direction.

That moment stayed with me. What felt ordinary to me had made a lasting impression on someone else. I didn't know I was influencing anyone. I was just being a kid. But even then, God was using my life, my environment, my joy, my presence to bless others without me trying.

As an adult, I see how that carries forward. I tend to isolate but influence still follows. I don't chase attention, yet people watch. I don't try to lead, but somehow, I do. That's grace. It's God positioning you to be light, even when you don't recognize the glow yourself.

Sometimes we overlook our impact because it feels natural to us. But what God places in you, your creativity, warmth, leadership, or joy, is never accidental. Influence isn't always loud. Sometimes it's simply showing up as yourself.

Scripture

"You are the light of the world. A city set on a hill cannot be hidden."

— Matthew 5:14

Reflection Questions

- What felt "normal" to you growing up that others saw as special?
- Where might God be using your influence without you realizing it?
- How can you embrace being a light without striving for attention?

Prayer

God, thank You for using me even when I don't see it. Help me recognize the quiet ways You work through my life and give me grace to walk confidently in the influence You've placed within me.

Amen.

THE HAPPY MEAL JOB

I laugh about it now, because it feels so small, but as a child, it felt big.

My mom had what I now know was a really good job. She worked at a school for children with special needs. On "Take Your Child to Work Day," I got to go with her, help, spend time with the residents, and even participate in things like the Special Olympics. I was exposed to compassion, patience, and service from an early age. At the time, I didn't see it that way. I just saw it as normal.

In elementary school, I had a friend whose mom worked at McDonald's. And to me, that was the dream job. Her mom would bring home Happy Meal toys, bags of them. We'd get the toys even without the meals. She could take her daughter to work, and they'd play in the Play Place. I was jealous. I remember telling my mom that my friend's mom had a better job than hers. Why? Because she brought home fun. Toys. Smiles. Things I could hold in my hands.

I didn't understand then that what my mom brought home couldn't fit inside a Happy Meal box. She brought home purpose. Stability. A heart for people who needed extra care. I couldn't see it because I was measuring value by what looked exciting, not by what was meaningful.

Now, as an adult, that memory humbles me. It reminds me how easy it is to overlook substance when we're distracted by surface-level rewards. Even now, we can fall into that same trap, thinking someone else's life, job, or calling is better because it looks more fun, more rewarding, or more visible. But God doesn't measure success the way we do.

Grace teaches us to see differently. To recognize that what may not look exciting at first glance might be shaping us and those around us in ways that matter far more than toys ever could.

Scripture

"'I have the right to do anything,' you say but not everything is beneficial."

— 1 Corinthians 10:23

Reflection Questions

- What did you value as a child that you now see differently as an adult?
- Where might you be comparing "fun" to "purpose" in your life today?
- How can you extend grace to yourself for what you didn't understand then?

Prayer

God, thank You for opening my eyes with time and maturity. Help me appreciate the deeper work you are doing in my life, even when it doesn't look exciting from the outside. Teach me to value purpose over appearances.

Amen.

BACK IN MY DAY

When I think back on it, we were really blessed.

My friends and I were part of a dance group called The Official Ladies. We competed in dance competitions. We opened for artists when they came to town. One of my friend's uncles owned a club, and during the day, when clubs were empty, he let us practice there. Downtown Pittsburgh became our second home.

We were young. Around thirteen. And we moved like adults.

We got on the bus ourselves. We practiced for hours. We used our own money. We fed ourselves dinner. Then we got back on the bus and went home. Every day. No supervision hovering. No phones tracking us. Just responsibility placed on our shoulders early.

A lot of us were raised helping raise someone else. I'm ten years older than my little sister. My friend had a similar age gap with her younger brother. Independence wasn't a choice; it was required. And somehow, we figured it out.

Now, as a parent, I look at my son and can't imagine him navigating the city alone at that age. I catch myself saying, "When I was younger, I had to…" But then I stop myself. Because while we carried responsibility early, we were also protected in ways kids today aren't.

We didn't have social media. We weren't comparing ourselves to fifteen-year-old millionaires online. We weren't absorbing body standards, lifestyles, and success stories from strangers on the internet. What we saw was what we saw in real life on the bus, at practice, at football games, or at house parties. Our world was smaller, but safer for our minds.

Today's kids are exposed to so much so early. Pressure doesn't wait anymore. Comparison is constant. And while their world looks easier on the surface, the weight they carry is heavier in ways we never had to experience.

Grace teaches me not to romanticize the past or criticize the present but to understand both. Every generation carries its own burdens. And wisdom comes from knowing how to protect, guide, and love through what's different, not just what's familiar.

Scripture

"For everything there is a season, and a time for every purpose under heaven."

— Ecclesiastes 3:1

Reflection Questions

- What responsibilities did you carry early that shaped who you are today?
- Where might comparison blind you to compassion for another generation?
- How can you extend grace to both your past and the present?

Prayer

God, help me honor where I came from without hardening my heart toward what's different. Give me wisdom to guide, protect, and love with understanding in every season.

Amen.

SECTION 2: THE STORIES THAT RAISED ME

LAUGHING SO I DON'T CRY

Some people think strength looks like never falling.

But real strength is getting back up laughing, so the fall doesn't get to own you.

Have you ever had one of those moments where life humbles you in front of everybody?

You feel cute.

Outfit on point.

Energy high.

You know you look good…

…and then life says, "Watch this."

This all-white boat party fall was one of those moments.

Picture this.

All white.

Feeling like that girl.

Wet steps.

Crowd on both levels.

Boom. Down the stairs.

In another version of me, that would've been tears.

Embarrassment.

Wanting to hide.

Energy ruined.

But the version of me I'm becoming knows something powerful:

If you laugh first, you don't give shame permission to speak.

When I laughed, the whole room relaxed.

The story changed from "look at her."

to "she's okay."

And more importantly, I was okay.

Sometimes laughing isn't denial.

It's survival.

Sometimes humor isn't avoidance.

It's emotional intelligence.

It's saying:

"Yeah, that was messy… but it didn't break me."

Because the truth is, life is full of slips.

Emotional slips.

Financial slips.

Relationship slips.

Public slips.

And if you let every fall define you, you'll stay stuck on the ground.

But when you learn to laugh, shake it off, and keep moving…

You take your power back.

You don't have to pretend it didn't hurt.

You just don't have to let it own you.

Scripture

"A joyful heart is good medicine, but a crushed spirit dries up the bones."

— Proverbs 17:22

Reflection

- When was the last time I laughed instead of spiraling?
- Do I allow myself to move past embarrassment?
- What would it look like to give myself more grace in awkward moments?

Prayer

God, help me not take myself so seriously that I forget to laugh. Teach me how to shake off what could've broken me. Let joy be my strength when life tries to embarrass me.

Amen.

THE HOUSE THAT NEVER SLEPT

If you grew up with your grandparents or spent real time in their home, then you know exactly what I mean.

My granddad lived just a few doors down from us. After he fainted and got out of the hospital, my mom didn't want him staying home alone. So we rotated nights staying with him. I stayed the most. My granddad and I were close.

He gave me his bedroom to sleep in and took the La-Z-Boy recliner in the living room. Even though I didn't mind sleeping in the recliner, he insisted. Looking back now, I realize how much that said about him. He always made room for me, even when it meant discomfort for himself.

He would wake up every morning around 4:30 a.m. and start cleaning. His house was already spotless, but that didn't stop him. One night, I noticed a mouse in the house. The same mouse kept showing up, and it terrified me. My granddad wasn't bothered at all. He said it would leave eventually. He knew his house was clean. But I was scared to even step on the floor.

So he adjusted for me.

Every time I stayed over, he cleaned even more. Vacuuming. Wiping walls. Making sure I felt safe. And because I was the "granddad babysitter," I had to be up with him at 4 a.m., too.

We'd eat breakfast around six and watch his shows, Days of Our Lives, the news, The Price Is Right, and old Westerns. His routine came first. Then we'd head to the store, and he'd jitney drive people home, what today would be Uber or Lyft. I helped load groceries, and at the end of the day, he'd slide me a few dollars.

At the time, I was just living it. Now I see it.

He didn't just want company, he wanted structure. He wanted purpose. He wanted me to feel safe. Even with the mouse. Even with the early mornings. Those moments meant more to him than I ever realized.

Grace lives in routines like that. In early mornings. In quiet sacrifice. In love that shows up consistently, not loudly. And now, I treasure those memories because they taught me that presence is sometimes the greatest gift we give.

Scripture

"Gray hair is a crown of splendor; it is attained in the way of righteousness."

— Proverbs 16:31

Reflection Questions

- What routines from your childhood now carry deeper meaning?
- Who showed love to you through consistency rather than words?
- How can you offer presence and structure to someone who needs it today?

Prayer

God, thank You for the people who loved me through routine, sacrifice, and quiet care. Help me honor those memories and carry that same steady love forward.

Amen.

THE SHOES THAT TAUGHT ME PERSPECTIVE

The teenage years were wild. Some of it looked like what you'd see on TV, and some of it you just can't document. One thing about my mom: she always wanted us to have nice things. She was the queen of "look for less." Marshalls. TJ Maxx. Burlington. Gabe's. Macy's clearance racks. She would search until she found the deal. And one thing she loved? Shoes.

That love made its way to us. Cute heels. Nice shoes. Things that made you feel confident walking into a room. I remember a pair of turquoise Nine West heels she bought me from Macy's. They were nice. Special. The kind of shoes you saved for the right occasion.

One of my friends was turning eighteen, and we were helping host her birthday party. The theme was Candy Shop, bright colors, bold looks. My assigned color was green, and I already had a pair of green heels picked out. But my friend didn't have a nice pair of shoes. So I let her borrow the turquoise heels.

After the party, I asked for them back. She kept dodging it. Circling around returning them. Then I saw her at the wave pool wearing them, which made no sense. Who wears heels to a wave pool? Then I saw her again at other events. Same shoes. Over and over. It became a joke. I even joked about it with my friends about how she was always going to have those shoes on.

I was annoyed. Hurt. A little mad. But eventually, something shifted. I realized she wasn't as fortunate as I was. Those shoes might've been the only nice pair she had. To me, what felt like entitlement was survival to her.

At the time, I didn't have the maturity to name it. But now I do. Grace doesn't always feel good in the moment. Sometimes it looks like letting go of something you feel entitled to when someone else truly needs it. The teen years taught me that belonging can blur the lines between sharing and sacrifice, and that understanding often comes later.

Scripture

"Do nothing out of selfish ambition or vain conceit. Rather, in humility value others above yourselves."

— Philippians 2:3

Reflection Questions

- Have you ever been upset in a moment that later revealed a deeper understanding?
- Where might perspective change how you view someone's actions today?
- What has maturity taught you about generosity and grace?

Prayer

God, help me see beyond my feelings in the moment and understand the hearts of others. Teach me to extend grace with wisdom and humility, even when it costs me something.

Amen.

WHEN ADULTS FORGET TO LEAD

When I look back on my childhood, I know now how blessed it really was. Even though there was poverty, it never felt like that. There were kids everywhere. We played outside all day. The neighborhood watched over us. I remember one time my little sister was somewhere she wasn't supposed to be, and the mailman walked her home. That's how covered we were. We didn't just have parents; we had a village.

But there's one memory that always stands out. There was a friend of mine whose aunt and family would sit on their porch and yell at us. They talked about us. Judged us. Made comments about the kids in the neighborhood. At the time, I didn't fully understand it. I just knew how it made us feel.

Now I'm the age they were back then. And that's what really gets me. I can't imagine sitting on a porch judging children instead of guiding them. I can't imagine looking at kids and seeing something to criticize rather than something to protect. I don't know if it came from jealousy, frustration, or something deeper, but I know it wasn't leadership.

That memory taught me something important: adults don't always get it right. And kids remember how you made them feel. We didn't need judgment; we needed direction. We didn't need commentary; we needed care.

Grace has shown me that who I choose to be now matters more than what I experienced then. I get to decide how I show up. I get to be the kind of adult I needed. And I get to lead with compassion instead of criticism.

Scripture

"Whoever welcomes one of these little children in my name welcomes me."

— Mark 9:37

Reflection Questions

- How did adults' words shape how you saw yourself as a child?
- What kind of example do you want to set for the next generation?
- Where might God be calling you to lead instead of judge?

Prayer

God, help me be the kind of adult who protects, guides, and uplifts. Heal the places where careless words once landed and teach me to lead with grace and compassion.

Amen.

LOYALTY AT ALL COST

If you grew up in a big neighborhood, you know what I mean when I say everyone felt like family. We weren't just friends, we were cousins, siblings, one big unit. You didn't move alone. You didn't stand alone. And you definitely didn't stay neutral.

Sometimes, kids from a few blocks over would come down, and things would turn into all-out brawls. It didn't always start with you. Sometimes it had nothing to do with you. But when it happened, there was an unspoken rule: loyalty mattered more than logic. If you weren't helping, you were hurting the group.

So you participated. You jumped in. Not because you were angry or violent, but because you didn't want to be separated afterward. You didn't want to be the one who didn't show up. Sitting out meant being pushed out. And for a teenager, losing your place in your community felt worse than getting hurt.

At the time, it felt like strength. Like unity. Like standing for something bigger than yourself. But looking back, I see how easily loyalty can turn into pressure. How belonging can quietly require you to abandon discernment. How fear of isolation can make you participate in things that don't align with who you really are.

Grace met me later with understanding. I learned that real loyalty doesn't demand you lose yourself. True belonging doesn't punish discernment. And God's version of community doesn't require you to fight battles that aren't yours just to stay connected.

Some lessons are learned in survival mode. Others are learned in reflection. Both deserve grace.

Scripture

"Do not follow the crowd in doing wrong."

— Exodus 23:2

Reflection Questions

- Have you ever felt pressured to participate just to belong?
- Where have you confused loyalty with obligation?
- What does a healthy community look like to you now?

Prayer

God, help me choose wisdom over pressure and truth over fear of being left out. Teach me to build and seek a community that reflects Your peace, not my insecurity.

Amen.

WHAT THE WATER COULDN'T WASH AWAY

I call it the big flood because, honestly, I still don't know where it came from.

We lived near what we called a creek, not a river, not a lake. Just a creek. We used to go down there, catching tadpoles and frogs, never really catching fish. It rained, and I remember waking up and looking out our front door. We lived at the top of the street, overlooking the housing projects below. Everything was underwater or becoming underwater fast.

The bottom row of houses was completely covered. You could only see the roofs. The homes higher up the slope were starting to go under too. My friends rushed down the hill because their grandfather lived there, and I went with them. When we got to his house, water was already pouring into the bottom floor. It was rising quickly. We were trying to get him out. But he refused to leave.

At the time, I couldn't understand it. Why wouldn't he leave? The water was coming in fast. His life was at risk. But the reason he gave stopped me. He didn't want to leave his home because his grandchildren's belongings were there. Their things. Their memories. He had already lost his wife, and what he was protecting wasn't furniture; it was pieces of their lives.

Back then, we didn't have social media or cloud storage. No flash drives. No backups. We had physical photos. Birth certificates. Important papers. And everyone knew you left those things with your grandparents because they didn't move as much. That house held history. Proof. Identity. He wasn't choosing possessions over life; he was choosing memory over erasure.

Eventually, we convinced him to leave after gathering what we could. But I still think about how firmly he stood. How willing he was to risk everything for what mattered most to him. As a child, I thought he was being stubborn. As an adult, I understand he was being human.

Grace taught me that day that value isn't always logical. People cling to what connects them to love, to legacy, to who they've lost. And sometimes what looks like resistance is really grief holding on to the only way it knows how.

Scripture

"Where your treasure is, there your heart will be also."

— Matthew 6:21

Reflection Questions

- What memories or moments would you struggle to leave behind?
- How has loss shaped what you value most?
- Where might grace be needed instead of judgment in understanding others' choices?

Prayer

God, help me see beyond surface decisions and understand the heart behind them. Teach me to value people, memories, and legacy with compassion, and to extend grace where I once questioned.

Amen.

LEFT IN THE MIDDLE

I still think about how crazy it was that this is how I learned to swim.

We had a neighborhood pool, and we were there from open to close. Sometimes I don't even remember us stopping to eat. All I wanted to do was play Gator. A game where someone stayed in the middle of the pool, and you had to swim past them before getting "eaten." But I couldn't swim across the middle. I stayed by the wall. Or I held onto the rope that stretched across the pool so I could pull myself along. I wanted to play, but fear kept me close to what felt safe.

So I asked my older sister and her friends to teach me how to swim. What I didn't know was how they planned to do it. The lifeguards were young teenagers, more like our friends than authority figures. My sister told them not to help me. One of her friends carried me out to the middle of the pool on her back. And then, without warning, she pried my hands off, swam away, and left me there.

I panicked. I was alone in the deep part of the pool. The lifeguard sat there laughing because he'd been told not to intervene. Everyone stood on the sidelines, cheering me on, telling me to focus, telling me I could do it. I didn't feel brave. I felt abandoned. But something in me kicked in. I had no choice but to move. And somehow, I swam.

That's how I learned. Not with gentle steps. Not with floaties. But by being left in the middle, I discovered I had more strength than I realized.

Looking back, I see how much of my life has mirrored that moment. God didn't always pull me out of deep water. Sometimes, he let me stay there long enough to learn I wouldn't drown. Sometimes the help I wanted didn't come the way I expected. But encouragement did. Growth did. Survival did.

Grace doesn't always rescue us from the middle. Sometimes it teaches us how to move through it.

Scripture

"When you pass through the waters, I will be with you… they will not sweep over you."

— Isaiah 43:2

Reflection Questions

- Where in your life have you felt left in the middle without a clear way out?
- How did that experience reveal a strength you didn't know you had?
- What would it look like to trust God even when the help you expect doesn't come immediately?

Prayer

God, help me trust You in the middle, not just at the edge where I feel safe. Remind me that even when I'm afraid, You are still with me, teaching me how to move forward.

Amen.

THE DAY I DIDN'T GO

There's a memory from my childhood that often comes back to me. I was about eight years old when my dad came to pick up my sister and me to take us to the Regatta in Pittsburgh. It's a big festival, art, food, games, booths, all the things' kids get excited about. That day, my dad didn't have much money. We did the free activities, grabbed McDonald's, and went home. I remember throwing a fit. I was embarrassed. I wanted to do what the other kids were doing. I didn't understand then what it took for him just to show up.

A few days later, he came back to get us again. This time, he had money. I was outside playing with my friends, enjoying the summer day, when my sister told me Dad was there to take us back. I said no. I didn't want to go. He even said, "I have money this time. You can get whatever you want." But I still refused. I could see it on his face that he was hurt, but I was stuck in how I felt from the first time. I chose my pride over the moment.

My dad passed away about two years after that. Now, as a single parent, that memory hits differently. I understand sacrifice in a way I couldn't back then. I understand how much it takes to create joy for your child when resources are limited. I understand how heavy it feels when your effort goes unseen. And I carry guilt not because I was a bad child, but because I didn't know how much that day meant to him.

But this is where grace steps in. I was a child. I didn't have the language or maturity to understand love expressed through effort rather than abundance. God has shown me that grace doesn't rewrite the past, but it heals how we hold it. That memory no longer exists to punish me; it exists to soften me. To remind me to show up differently. To extend grace to my child. And to extend grace to myself.

Scripture

"The Lord is compassionate and gracious, slow to anger, abounding in love."

— Psalm 103:8

Reflection Questions

- Is there a childhood memory you carry guilt over that needs grace instead of judgment?
- How has your perspective changed now that you understand sacrifice more deeply?
- What would it look like to forgive your younger self today?

Prayer

God, thank You for meeting me with grace where guilt once lived. Help me release what I couldn't understand back then and teach me to love myself the way You do fully and without condition.

Amen.

WHEN NOTHING REGISTERED

When I think about my dad's passing, what stands out the most is how fast everything happened and how little I understood in the moment. One minute, I was outside playing with my friends. Next, my mom was pulling us together and saying we had to go to the hospital. When we arrived, his entire family was in the room. He was in the bed, surrounded by people, and when my sister and I walked in, the room fell silent. I could feel the weight of it, but I didn't know what it meant.t.

My mom walked us up to his bedside. No one explained that this would be the last time I would see my dad breathing. I didn't know he had suffered a brain aneurysm or that he was already considered brain dead. I didn't understand that everyone was there to say goodbye before life support was removed. I loved my dad deeply. I was a true daddy's girl, but my mind couldn't process what my heart was about to lose. I felt numb. I knew I was supposed to be sad, but I didn't know why.

Even after leaving the hospital, I went back to playing with my friends. Later, my mom came to get me and told me my dad had passed. I remember her face more than her words. She looked crushed. Still, it didn't register. At the funeral, my sister and I were dressed in all white. All eyes were on us. We were the center of attention, and I felt… nothing. I couldn't connect to the moment. The grief didn't come then. It waited. It showed up later in the absence. In the times my dad didn't pull up just to hang out. In the way, he wasn't there when we went to my grandmother's house, helping us navigate a sea of cousins. In watching my best friend grow up with her dad present. In realizing how different things might have felt if that male figure had stayed. I had my granddad for a time, but he passed away too. And just like that, the presence I didn't know how to grieve was gone. Looking back now, I understand that numbness was not weakness, it was protection. God shielded me until I had the capacity to feel it. Grief doesn't always arrive loud and immediate. Sometimes it waits until you're strong enough to carry it. And grace meets you wherever it shows up.

Scripture

"The Lord is close to the brokenhearted and saves those who are crushed in spirit."

— Psalm 34:18

Reflection Questions

- Have you ever felt numb during a loss you didn't fully understand at the time?
- Where has grief shown up later in your life rather than immediately?
- What would it look like to give yourself grace for how you survived?

Prayer

God, thank You for staying close even when I didn't understand what I was losing. Heal the places where absence shaped me and help me trust that You fill every gap with Your presence.

Amen.

THE FACE OF GRIEF

The neighborhood I grew up in felt like the best place on earth. Every house had kids, and we were always outside playing, laughing, running through each other's yards like one big family. It felt safe. It felt blessed. Until it wasn't.

One day, while we were outside playing, a shooting happened. My friend's mom was standing just a few feet away from me when she was hit by a stray bullet. She passed away right there, in front of us. I was a child, and in a single moment, innocence shifted. Death was no longer something distant or abstract. It was right in front of us, woven into a place that once felt untouchable.

What stayed with me just as much as her passing was what came after. Watching her spouse try to survive without her. He drank constantly outside, openly, almost as if alcohol was the only way he knew how to breathe through the pain. As a child, I didn't have the words for it. As an adult, I understand it was grief without tools. Pain without support. Loss without direction.

That moment taught me how quickly life can change. It also showed me how trauma doesn't stop with the person who's gone; it ripples through families, friendships, and entire communities. I think about the effect that loss had on my friends, on their home, on the way they had to grow up faster than they should have.

But grace shows up even here. Not by erasing what happened, but by teaching me compassion. I learned early that people cope the best way they know how, even when it's unhealthy, even when it's messy. And I learned that God is still present in the hardest moments, even when we don't recognize Him then.

Some lessons arrive too early. But grace meets us there, too.

Scripture

"The righteous person may have many troubles, but the lord delivers him from them all."

— Psalm 34:19

Reflection Questions

- Have you experienced loss earlier in life than you were prepared for?
- How has witnessing grief shaped your compassion for others?
- Where might God be inviting you to extend grace to someone who is coping imperfectly?

Prayer

God, You see the moments that shaped me before I had the words to understand them. Heal the places where trauma entered too early and help me walk in compassion for those who grieve without knowing how.

Amen.

SECTION 3: MAMA MODE

CARRYING HIM ALONE

Having a child is hard.

Having a child when it feels like you're alone is even harder.

While I was pregnant, I carried more than a baby; I carried the weight of knowing I was about to raise a man by myself. I was bringing a son into the world alone. And I didn't know what that life would look like. I didn't have a blueprint. I just had fear, responsibility, and faith, which I was still learning how to use.

I found myself going to church more during that season. Every altar call, I was there. Not because I had the words, but because I needed guidance. I needed reassurance. I needed God to show me what my life was becoming. I didn't fully understand faith then, but I knew who to call on.

When my son was born, people came to the hospital. They celebrated. They held him. And then they left. And suddenly, it was just me and this tiny human I was now fully responsible for. I took him home at twenty-two years old, trying to learn how to breastfeed, how to soothe him, how to provide, how to protect him. He had colic. I was exhausted. Overwhelmed. Learning everything in real time.

There was resentment back then. I wanted the other person involved to feel what I felt, to carry what I carried. I wanted them to see my son the way I saw him. To want him so badly they couldn't breathe without him. But that wasn't what God had planned.

Over time, something shifted. God provided everything I needed. And more. People told me I should fight, sue, and demand help. And while they may have been right, my response stayed the same: I've been so blessed. My son and I have always had more than enough. God has kept us this entire time.

I don't move from bitterness. I move from grace. I don't carry hatred. I carry understanding. I can forgive without presence. I can release without closure. And I can move forward knowing that this journey raising my son on my own was not a punishment. It was a calling.

This is what was intended for me.

And God has been faithful every step of the way.

Scripture

"God sets the lonely in families; He leads out the prisoners with singing."

— Psalm 68:6

Reflection Questions

- Where have you been asked to carry something heavier than you expected?
- How has God provided for you in ways that replaced resentment with peace?
- What would it look like to trust that your journey, even the hard parts, has purpose?

Prayer

God, thank You for meeting me in moments I thought I couldn't survive. Help me continue to walk in forgiveness, strength, and trust, knowing that You are the provider, protector, and author of my story.

Amen.

FOR SUCH A TIME AS THIS

Esther didn't ask to be chosen. She didn't ask to be placed in a position where her voice could change everything.

But God did.

She was a woman in a world where women weren't protected like that. She was trying to survive. Trying to stay safe. Trying not to make the wrong move. And then life demanded something bigger from her: courage.

What I love about Esther is that she didn't pretend she wasn't scared. She didn't act like faith meant she felt no fear. She literally said, if I perish, I perish.

That's real.

Because sometimes obedience doesn't feel like confidence. Sometimes it feels like shaking hands, racing thoughts, a tight chest… and still doing it anyway.

Some of us are waiting to feel "ready" before we speak up.

Before we start.

Before we leave.

Before we set the boundary.

Before we choose ourselves.

Before we step into purpose.

But Esther teaches us: you don't wait until you're fearless. You move while you're afraid with God.

You may be the only one in your family who's breaking cycles.

You may be the only one at your job who's standing on integrity.

You may be the only one in your friend group who's truly changing.

You may be the only one your child is watching.

That's not pressure. That's purpose.

You are not "randomly here."

You are positioned.

Scripture

"And who knows but that you have come to your royal position for such a time as this?" — Esther 4:14

Reflection Questions

- Where is God asking me to be brave right now?
- What conversation am I avoiding because it's uncomfortable?
- What would I do if I believed I was positioned on purpose?

Prayer

God, give me Esther courage, not the kind that feels fearless, but the kind that moves anyway. Help me stop shrinking when You've called me to stand. Use my life, my voice, and my obedience for such a time as this. In Jesus' name, amen.

SELFLESS PARENTING

It feels like a small memory, but it changed everything for me.

My son was about three or four years old. I was tired. It was late. Money was tight. Everything I had at home was frozen, and I didn't feel like cooking. I thought a $5 pizza would be an easy option, something we could both eat. But he didn't want pizza. He cried and cried for McDonald's. He didn't understand that pizza was the option that fed both of us. He was just a child who wanted what he wanted.

I remember trying to reason with him. "Pizza, dude. We can both eat pizza."

But he didn't get it. And how could he? He was three.

So I got him the McDonald's.

And I didn't eat.

When we got home, I made myself noodles. I didn't think much of it in the moment; I'd done what moms do. I chose him. But that night stayed with me. Because for the first time, I realized what it meant to choose between providing joy for my child and nourishing myself.

At first, I felt upset. I remember thinking, How could he be so selfish?

And then reality settled in, he wasn't selfish. He was a child. The weight of the moment wasn't his to carry. It was mine.

That night, I made a quiet promise to myself: I will never be here again.

Not because I was ashamed. Not because I failed. But because I understood something had to change. Love will always choose sacrifice, but grace taught me that survival doesn't have to stay that way forever.

God met me in that resolve. He didn't shame me for the noodles. He strengthened me for what came next. That moment didn't define my lack; it defined my determination.

Scripture

"The Lord is my shepherd; I shall not want."

— Psalm 23:1

Reflection Questions

- Have you ever made a quiet sacrifice that no one else noticed?
- What moments have shaped your determination to build something different?
- How can you honor your past sacrifices without living in them?

Prayer

God, thank You for meeting me in the moments no one saw. Strengthen me where I once had to choose between survival and sacrifice and help me trust You as the provider for what comes next.

Amen.

TRYING TO MAKE UP FOR THE HOURS

As parents, we want our kids to have everything we didn't have.

We want them to feel loved, secure, and provided for. And for a long time, I tried to do that the only way I knew how, by overcompensating.

I worked constantly. My son was around three years old when this became our routine. In the middle of the night, I'd wrap him up in blankets and jackets and take him with me from office building to office building while I cleaned. Alone. He would sleep on a chair, or I'd push two chairs together, or let him lie on a desk. Sometimes he'd wake up and want to help empty trash, carry something small, or feel useful in his own little way. Other nights, I'd set him up with an iPad on a desk and let him be there while I worked through the night.

That was our reality.

And when we weren't working toward my goals, I tried to make up for what I felt he was missing. I bought him things. I threw him the biggest birthday parties. People would come just because his parties were known to be the parties. I spent thousands of dollars trying to fill the gaps, trying to compensate for the long hours, the late nights, the absence of a consistent father figure, and the fact that his childhood didn't always look soft or simple.

I carried guilt. Guilt that he had to grow up a little faster. Guilt that instead of being warm at home on cold, snowy nights, he was helping Mommy clean buildings. Guilt that survival demanded flexibility from a child who deserved ease.

But grace met me there, too.

I see now that what I thought was overcompensation was really love trying to find expression under pressure. I wasn't absent, I was present in the only way I could be at the time. And God covered the parts I couldn't. He always does.

That season taught me something important: children don't need perfection; they need presence, honesty, and love that shows up even when it's tired. And parents deserve grace for the seasons where survival looks different than the dream.

Scripture

"Love bears all things, believes all things, hopes all things, endures all things."

— 1 Corinthians 13:7

Reflection Questions

- Where have you tried to compensate for something you felt guilty about?
- How might grace re-frame what you once viewed as failure or lack?
- What does presence look like for you in this season of life?

Prayer

God, thank You for seeing my heart when my circumstances were heavy. Help me release guilt for the seasons where survival demanded more than comfort, and remind me that love, imperfect but faithful, still counts.

Amen.

LOOKING LIKE I HAD IT TOGETHER

For a few years, my son's father and sometimes his family would show up to his birthday parties. Not consistently. Not to help. But because my son's birthdays were the place to be.

And I made sure of that.

I threw big, extravagant parties. I'm talking about taking 30+ kids to another state for an overnight stay at an indoor water park, including breakfast, lunch, and dinner. Renting indoor arenas for kickball parties. Creating experiences that were nothing like the typical pizza party or Chuck E. Cheese. My son's parties were creative, intentional, and unforgettable.

People loved them.

And I'll be honest; those parties were about more than celebration. They were my message. To his dad. To his family. To anyone who might look at me and see a single mom and assume struggle. My message was simple: We're good. I don't need help. I've got this.

Whether they showed up or just heard about it, I wanted them to know I was making it happen with or without them. I wanted them to see that my son was well taken care of. That I had it all figured out.

But behind the scenes, it was a grind.

I worked harder than anyone saw to pull those parties off. It wasn't effortless. It wasn't easy. It was pressure. It was late nights. It was stretching myself thin to make sure everything looked full.

That season taught me something important: sometimes we perform well because we're tired of being underestimated. Sometimes extravagance is armor. And sometimes what looks like confidence is actually survival, trying to stand tall.

Grace met me there, too. It reminded me that I don't have to prove anything to anyone. My worth as a mother isn't measured by how impressive the celebration looks. My son didn't need proof; he needed presence. And I was already giving him that.

Scripture

"Man looks at the outward appearance, but the Lord looks at the heart."

— 1 Samuel 16:7

Reflection Questions

- Where have you felt the need to prove you're okay instead of admitting you're tired?
- How has performance masked pressure in your life?
- What would it look like to rest in truth instead of presentation?

Prayer

God, help me let go of the need to prove myself. Remind me that you see the work no one else sees and that my value isn't tied to how put-together I appear. Teach me to rest in Your approval alone.

Amen.

WHEN HIS STRUGGLES FEEL LIKE FAILURE

Nothing breaks my heart more than when my son isn't doing well in school.

I already feel the weight when I show up. Showing up alone. Showing up in work clothes. Showing up to sporting events and school functions where it's clear who came with two parents and who didn't. Dads over here. Moms helping at the concession stand. And I'm just there doing my best, carrying everything quietly.

So when my son starts struggling academically, it hits differently.

It makes me feel like I've failed him.

Not because I'm absent. Not because I don't love him or know him. But because I'm tired. Because I'm working two jobs. Because every sacrifice I've made, every late night, every boundary, every ounce of energy has been to put him in the best possible position. I work the way I do, so we can live in this area. So he can go to good schools. So he can have opportunities I didn't.

And when he doesn't perform at the level I know he's capable of, because he is bright, it breaks me.

I find myself thinking, I worked so hard to get you here. The least you can do is show up the way you're supposed to.

And then grace steps in.

Because I have to remember that this move was hard for him too. That being away from family affects him in ways I may not always see. Social media makes growing up harder than when I was his age. That children feel pressure even when they don't have the language for it. And still, grace doesn't mean lowering expectations. It means leading with love instead of frustration.

I'm learning that I can hold him accountable and still hold him gently. That I can want more for him without turning his struggle into my shame. His grades don't define my worth as a mother or his worth as a child.

God keeps reminding me that parenting isn't about perfection. It's about patience. About showing up again and again, even when your heart feels heavy. Especially then.

Scripture

"Fathers, do not exasperate your children; instead, bring them up in the training and instruction of the Lord."

— Ephesians 6:4

Reflection Questions

- Where have you tied your worth to someone else's performance?
- How can you extend grace without releasing responsibility?
- What might God be teaching you and your child through this season?

Prayer

God, help me separate my identity from outcomes I can't fully control. Teach me how to parent with patience, wisdom, and grace. Strengthen my heart when disappointment creeps in and remind me that You are at work in both of us, even when progress feels slow. Amen.

LET THEM BE LITTLE

We were all sitting at my friend's grandmother's house, talking and laughing, when my son kept saying he had to go to the bathroom.

"Go ahead inside," I told him.

A few seconds later, I heard my friend's uncle yell,

"Junior!"

We all turned... and there was my four-year-old, standing by a tree, little booty out, peeing like he was out in the wilderness.

My first feeling was pure second-hand embarrassment.

Like, oh my God... this is not how I raised you.

But my friend's uncle was proud.

"That's a boy," he said. "That's what he's supposed to do."

And in that moment, something clicked.

We spend so much time trying to raise perfect, polite, well-mannered, Instagram-ready kids that we forget they are still just... kids.

Sometimes they're loud.

Sometimes they're messy.

Sometimes they do things that make you want to hide your face. But they're also innocent.

They're learning.

They're just being who God created them to be.

Not everything needs to be corrected.

Not everything needs to be shamed.

Not every moment has to be "proper."

Some moments just need grace.

Scripture

"Start children off on the way they should go, and even when they are old they will not turn from it."

— Proverbs 22:6

Reflection Questions

- Am I expecting my child (or myself) to be too grown too soon?
- Do I leave room for innocence, mistakes, and learning?
- How do I react when things don't go the way I imagined?

Prayer

God, help me give grace in the little moments.

Remind me that growth is messy, learning is awkward, and childhood is sacred.

Teach me not to rush perfection in my kids or in myself.

Let me lead with patience, laughter, and love.

Thank you for the joy that comes in the unexpected moments.

Amen.

MEETING THEM WHERE THEY ARE

Meeting people where they are is powerful.

But meeting kids where they are? That takes patience, humility, and real grace.

I have to remind myself often not to start sentences with, "When I was your age…"

Because the truth is, when I was younger, the world was different.

Yes, we worked harder in some ways.

Yes, we had responsibilities early.

But we didn't have TikTok.

We didn't have Instagram.

We didn't have social media in the palms of our hands, reminding us every second that we might not be enough.

Back then, comparison was limited. You saw a few celebrities on TV. Maybe some popular kids at school. If you didn't have the latest shoes or clothes, it wasn't broadcast to millions of people daily. It wasn't algorithm driven. It wasn't constant.

Today's kids are carrying pressure we never had to name.

They're watching kids their age become millionaires overnight.

They're seeing influencers travel the world, get free things, and live lavish lives before they've even figured out who they are.

They're bombarded with ads, expectations, beauty standards, and success narratives 24/7.

And if we as adults struggle not to feel behind, imagine being 14.

Imagine trying to figure out your identity while the world is telling you what you should look like, own, earn, and achieve before you even graduate high school. That's heavy.

So I've learned to give kids grace.

To meet them where they are mentally, emotionally, and socially. To understand that their struggles may look different from ours, but they're no less real. To stop minimizing their experiences just because they don't mirror our own.

Grace doesn't mean lowering expectations.

It means leading with empathy.

It means recognizing that this generation is navigating a mentally challenging world and needs guidance, not judgment. They need reassurance, not comparison. They need adults who listen rather than dismiss.

Because if it's hard for us to navigate this world with fully developed brains, then kids deserve compassion while they're learning how to do the same.

Scripture

"Be completely humble and gentle; be patient, bearing with one another in love."

— Ephesians 4:2

Reflection Questions

- Where have you compared someone's journey to your own without considering their environment?
- How can you show more empathy to younger generations navigating pressures you didn't face?
- What does meeting someone where they are look like in practice?

Prayer

God, help me lead with understanding instead of comparison. Give me patience to meet others, especially children, where they are, and wisdom to guide them with love in a world that demands so much from them.

Amen.

CHOOSING BLESSED OVER WORRIED

It's become a running joke to people around me who aren't as invested in their relationship with God.

They ask, "How are you doing?"

I say, "Blessed."

"How's your day going?"

"I'm blessed."

"How do you feel about this situation?"

"I'm blessed."

And I mean it.

No matter what's going on, I'm intentional with my words. I don't lead with exhaustion. I don't lead with stress. I don't lead with lack. I choose to speak life because words shape reality.

It shocks people sometimes. They say things like, "You're always in good spirits." And it's not because life is perfect, it's because I refuse to let my circumstances control my confession.

There are days I have every reason to complain. Bills due. Stress at work. Worry about my child. Fatigue. Pressure. But I've learned something important: worry is not trusting God.

And I don't owe everyone access to my struggles.

Not everyone who asks how you're doing actually care. Some people are fishing. Some are looking for weakness. Some want confirmation that you're struggling too. So I protect my spirit. I don't lie, but I also don't give energy to negativity.

Saying "I'm blessed" doesn't mean I don't have problems.

It means I trust God more than I trust my feelings.

By changing how I speak, I changed how I think.

By changing how I think, I changed how I move.

And by changing how I move, I changed how people see me.

It may sound repetitive. It may sound like a joke. But it's intentional.

Because the life I speak over myself is the life I'm choosing to live, whether anyone else likes it or not.

Scripture

"Do not be anxious about anything, but in every situation, by prayer and petition, with thanksgiving, present your requests to God."

— Philippians 4:6

Reflection Questions

- What do your words reveal about what you truly believe?
- Where has worry been louder than faith in your life?
- How might your environment change if you consistently spoke life?

Prayer

God, help me guard my words and trust You fully. Teach me to speak faith over fear, gratitude over worry, and life over every situation I face.

Amen.

THE HEALING DRIVE

Sometimes the best therapy doesn't come from a couch.

It comes from a long road.

There is something sacred about getting in your car, grabbing your favorite warm drink, turning on a playlist (or turning everything off), and just driving. No destination. No performance. Just you and your thoughts.

That's where emotional security is built.

Not when someone else tells you who you are…

But when you sit with yourself long enough to listen.

A long drive gives you space to process what you've been avoiding:

Maybe now isn't your time to have another child.

Maybe that relationship didn't work because it wasn't meant to.

Maybe your child needs a deeper conversation.

Maybe you need to forgive yourself for something you haven't let go of yet.

You can play the scenarios out.

You can be honest without being judged.

You can cry.

You can laugh.

You can remember.

You can plan.

And in that space, you begin to understand:

Not everything that didn't happen was a failure.

Some things didn't happen because you were being protected.

Sometimes you don't need opinions.

You need clarity.

And clarity often comes when you slow down long enough to hear your own heart and God's whisper.

There is joy in the small things:

A warm drink.

A favorite song.

A peaceful stretch of road.

A moment where you feel safe inside yourself.

That's where healing starts.

Scripture

"He refreshes my soul. He guides me along the right paths for his name's sake."

— Psalm 23:3

Reflection

- What is something I've been avoiding thinking about?
- If I were honest with myself, what would I admit right now?
- What part of my life needs clarity instead of noise?
- What small joy can I intentionally create for myself today?

Prayer

God, thank You for meeting me in the quiet.

Thank you for being present when I slow down enough to listen.

Help me be honest with myself without shame.

Give me clarity where I feel confused,

peace where I feel anxious,

and the courage to accept what is and trust what's coming.

Teach me how to feel safe inside my own heart.

Amen.

SECTION 4: LOVE LESSONS

SHE DOES IT ANYWAY

As women, we carry so much, and a lot of it is invisible.

Even something as normal as being on your cycle… cramps, pain, hormones everywhere, and you still get up and handle life like nothing's wrong. Still clock in. Still show up. Still parent. Still answer texts. Still smile at strangers in the grocery store. Still crack jokes at work. Still make it happen.

And sometimes you're not just tired, you're anxious. You're low. You're carrying quite a sadness. But you don't always have time to unpack it because the day is already mapped out in your head:

Work from this time to this time.

Stop at the store at this time.

Back home with just enough minutes to cook before your son gets home.

If there's a second job, you go.

If there isn't, you're catching up on laundry, dishes, cleaning, homework, and life.

And in the middle of all that, you're still being present for everybody else.

People ask, "How do you do it?" and we'll say, "I don't know… I just do."

But the truth is, it's not luck.

It's not luck that you made it through the day.

It's not luck that you keep pushing.

It's not luck that you're doing the impossible with a straight face.

It's God, and it's the strength He put in you.

Many women struggle with imposter syndrome. We second-guess ourselves. We minimize our wins like they "just happened" or like we "just got lucky." But no, you didn't stumble into survival. You didn't accidentally become capable. You didn't fall into being consistent.

God graced you. And you showed up.

Some days it feels like you have more hours than everybody else because somehow you still manage to get it all done, lie down, sleep, and wake up and do it again.

So if nobody told you today, making it through is an accomplishment.

Not because you "got lucky," but because you're built for this and God is carrying you through it.

SCRIPTURE

"I can do all this through him who gives me strength."

— Philippians 4:13

REFLECT

- What am I carrying right now that nobody sees?
- Where have I mistaken God's strength in me for "just luck"?
- What is one way I can give myself grace today?

PRAYER

God, thank You for carrying me through the days I don't talk about. Thank You for the strength You put in me to show up even when my body is tired, my mind is heavy, and my emotions are all over the place. Help me stop minimizing what You've done in me and through me. Teach me to receive help, to rest without guilt, and to give myself grace while I'm still becoming. In Jesus' name,

Amen.

WHAT LOOKED LIKE A BLESSING

I remember watching other women and their relationships.

They had the purses, the clothes, the shoes, the trips, the jewelry. From the outside, it looked like love. It looked like security. And I wanted that. I wanted to be chosen. I wanted to be spoiled. So I prayed for it.

I prayed for a man who would buy me things. Take me on trips. Provide. Spoil me.

And God answered that prayer exactly as I asked.

I got the man. We built a business together. I lived in a nice home. From the outside looking in, everything was perfect. But behind closed doors, he was a monster. He abused me physically, mentally, and emotionally. Bruised ribs. Chipped teeth. Staples in my head. Fear that lived in my body. And then he'd walk outside and smile like nothing was wrong.

I endured that life for two years.

I didn't leave because I was weak. I stayed because I was human. Because I was a nurturer. Because somehow, someway, he always found a way back through sympathy, through pain, through stories that pulled on my compassion. And not just fear kept me there. I didn't want him to hurt the way I was hurting. I didn't want my abuser to suffer. That's how twisted love can become when it's mixed with trauma.

I knew I didn't have the strength to leave on my own. So I prayed a different prayer.

I would be on my hands and knees in the bathroom when he wasn't looking, begging God:

Please remove this person from my life. Please. Because I can't do it myself.

And God did.

That season taught me something I will never forget, never envy what looks good on the outside. You never know what someone is surviving behind closed doors. What looks like provision can be a prison. And what you ask for without discernment can cost you more than you ever imagined.

Grace taught me to trust God's will over my own desires. Because He sees what we can't and He loves us enough to rescue us when we finally ask.

Scripture

"Each one should test their own actions... without comparing themselves to someone else, for each one should carry their own load."

— Galatians 6:4-5

Reflection Questions

- Have you ever prayed for something that later revealed a hidden cost?
- Where might envy be clouding discernment in your life today?
- What would it look like to trust God's protection over outward appearances?

Prayer

God, forgive me for the times I wanted what looked good instead of what was good for me. Thank you for rescuing me when I didn't have the strength to rescue myself. Help me trust Your will above my desires and walk forward in freedom and wisdom.

Amen.

AFRAID TO LET GO

Not trusting God's plan for my life kept me in places that were hurting me.

I stayed in an abusive relationship out of fear, fear of letting him be with someone else. I allowed cheating. I allowed physical abuse. Mental abuse. Emotional abuse. Because somewhere deep inside, I believed that if I didn't accept those things, he would go give himself to another woman. And as painful as it was, I told myself it was better if he stayed, even if it cost me my peace.

When I think about it now, it sounds unreal. But fear doesn't think clearly. Fear convinces you that what's hurting you is still yours to protect. That letting go means losing something valuable. When in reality, what you're holding onto is harming you.

I was young. And I didn't understand then what I understand now: let them have it.

Let them have the chaos. Let them have the pain. Let them have what looks good on the outside but is destructive on the inside. And pray honestly that no one else has to endure what you endured.

The lesson didn't come quickly. It took time. It took exhaustion. It took me reaching a breaking point. And finally, it took trusting God enough to let Him remove what I didn't have the strength to release on my own.

After that relationship ended for good, God taught me something unexpected: the power of being alone. I didn't date. I didn't rush into anything new. I sat by myself. With the silence. With the healing. And that solitude gave me strength I never had before.

Some people jump from relationship to relationship because they don't know how to sit alone. But being alone taught me my worth. It taught me peace. It taught me that genuine connection should never require self-abandonment.

I don't regret the growth. I don't glorify the pain. I understand now that I had to walk through that season to become someone who wants love without losing herself.

Scripture

"God has not given us a spirit of fear, but of power, love, and a sound mind."

— 2 Timothy 1:7

Reflection Questions

- Where has fear kept you holding onto something that was hurting you?
- What does being alone reveal about your sense of worth?
- How can trusting God help you release what no longer serves you?

Prayer

God, thank You for removing what I was too afraid to let go of. Teach me to trust You over fear and to value peace over possessions. Help me continue to walk in strength, clarity, and self-worth.

Amen.

WHEN EVERYTHING WAS TAKEN

One of the most freeing moments of my life came wrapped in one of the most terrifying experiences.

After God removed my abuser from my life, my home was burglarized. I had left to pick up my son from daycare, stopped by my mom's house and the grocery store, and came back about two hours later. As I walked up to my apartment, I immediately felt something was wrong.

I lived in what I thought was a secure place. A brand-new luxury apartment complex. Professional athletes lived there. The police chief lived there. It felt untouchable. But because I lived on the ground level, someone jumped the banister, broke the glass on the back door, and let themselves in.

My front door was unlocked.

I stopped my son and told him to wait. I pushed the door open just enough to see that everything was destroyed. Furniture flipped. Sliced. Drawers emptied. Every room, bedroom, kitchen, laundry room, trashed. I didn't go any further. I grabbed my son, ran down the hallway to the mailroom, and called the police. Then my mom. Then my best friend. We waited.

When I was finally able to go back inside, I realized something else: everything my abuser had given me was gone. Purses. Jewelry. Gifts meant for my mom and his mom. All of it. The things that once made me look like that girl. The things I had prayed for. The things that came at such a high cost.

In the moment, I was devastated.

My son and I were terrified. We couldn't sleep in our bedroom. We slept together on the couch every night, staring at the boarded-up back door. The complex wasn't supportive. The police weren't gentle. I felt like I was being treated as a suspect instead of a victim. Someone even told me it had to be someone who knew me, because no one else's apartment had been touched.

That thought stayed with me.

When I asked to break my lease, the complex refused. They wanted three months' rent, nearly five figures. I was overwhelmed. Exhausted. Still healing. Still afraid. I pushed back. I wrote. I explained. And eventually, they let me out of the lease.

And that moment that release changed everything.

That home was tied to pain. To fear. To a version of me that survived but wasn't free. And suddenly, all the things that connected me to that chapter were gone. Taken. And somehow, that loss became my freedom.

God stripped away what I couldn't let go of on my own. And in doing so, He gave me a clean start. Not just a new home but a new beginning for my son and me.

Scripture

"But whatever were gains to me I now consider loss for the sake of Christ… I consider them garbage, that I may gain Christ."

— Philippians 3:7-8

Reflection Questions

- What have you lost that later created space for freedom?
- Are there things tying you to a past season God may be asking you to release?
- What would a fresh start look like for you right now?

Prayer

God, thank You for protecting me even in moments of fear and loss. Help me trust You when things are stripped away and remind me that new beginnings often come disguised as endings.

Amen.

WATCHING FROM THE OUTSIDE

Social media can be a hard place to exist, especially when you're raising a child alone. It gives you access to people's lives without the closeness, context, or truth. And for me, watching my son's father live his life traveling, breathing freely, and moving on while not being present in our child's life struck a nerve.

At the time, it hurt deeply. Not because I wanted his life, but because I was in the trenches. I was raising a child I didn't make alone. I was showing up every day emotionally, financially, spiritually, while watching someone else move through life without acknowledging the responsibility that existed here with me. And when things were hard, when I was struggling in ways people didn't see, there was no offer of help. No check-in. No presence.

Over time, God began to shift my perspective. I started asking myself a hard question: Is this even the kind of man I would want shaping my child's values? Forgiveness came slowly, but it came. Not because the pain disappeared but because I realized this wasn't a battle for me to fight. It was between him and God.

I learned that what looks good on the outside doesn't always reflect what's happening on the inside. Social media only shows highlights, not character. And I had to learn to disconnect from what I was seeing online and stay grounded in what was real. The real work. The real love. The real sacrifice is happening right in front of me.

God clearly placed it on my heart: You can forgive without forcing access.

I don't have to demand a relationship that someone doesn't want. I don't have to chase presence. I get to choose peace. I get to choose genuine love for my son, love that shows up willingly, consistently, and fully. That lesson wasn't easy. But it was freeing.

Scripture

"Let all bitterness and wrath and anger be put away from you… forgiving one another, as God in Christ forgave you."

— Ephesians 4:31–32

Reflection Questions

- How has social media comparison affected your healing?
- Where might forgiveness be freeing you more than the other person?
- What does genuine love and presence look like in your life today?

Prayer

God, help me release what I cannot control and trust You with what I don't understand. Teach me to forgive without bitterness and to surround my life with real, present, and sincere love. Teach me what love truly looks like. Patient, kind, honest, and safe. A love that reflects you. Cover me in discernment and fill me with peace. Align me with love that is genuine, mutual, and lasting. In Jesus name,

Amen

LEARNING HOW TO RECEIVE LOVE

When I moved to Georgia, I immediately got into a relationship.

And in many ways, it felt perfect.

He was gentle, completely opposite of what I had known before. He never raised his voice. He was patient, kind, and emotionally present. I got flowers delivered every week. Constant reassurance. Thoughtfulness in ways I didn't even know I needed. One time, he noticed a blanket I'd had since my son was born had a small tear. He quietly took it to the dry cleaners and had it stitched. I walked into rooms fully decorated. I was loved openly, intentionally, consistently.

It was everything people say they want.

And still, I struggled.

He was emotional in ways that overwhelmed me. He wanted closeness all the time. If I went into another room, even when nothing was wrong, it hurt his feelings. And I didn't know how to explain that my need for space wasn't rejection. It was survival. I had learned how to be alone. How to sit in silence. How to not talk to anyone. And at that point in my life, I worked jobs where I talked to people all day. When I came home, I needed quiet to decompress.

He wanted to be close. I wanted space.

Neither of us was wrong; we were just different. Raised differently. Wired differently. Loving differently. And I didn't yet know how to fully receive the kind of affection he was offering. My life had hardened me. I didn't grow up in a family that said "I love you" every day. That softness came later with my son, who is naturally affectionate and expressive. Loving him taught me how to say the words and give the hugs.

That relationship didn't last, but it taught me something invaluable. It taught me how to soften. How to recognize healthy affection. How to see that love doesn't have to hurt to be real. And it also taught me that honoring my need for space matters too.

Now, years later, I find myself in a different situation, one where the roles are reversed. Where I crave affection, and the other person needs space. And it's shown me how important communication is. How clearly knowing what you need and being able to say it can change everything.

God gives us what we need in each season. In that season, I needed to learn how to receive love without fear. How to soften without losing myself. How to grow without forcing permanence.

And that lesson stayed with me.

Scripture

"Above all, love each other deeply, because love covers over a multitude of sins."

— 1 Peter 4:8

Reflection Questions

- How do you give and receive love differently than others?
- Where has your past shaped your ability to accept affection or closeness?
- What would it look like to communicate your needs with both honesty and grace?

Prayer

God, help me recognize the lessons You place in each season. Teach me how to receive love without fear, honor my needs without guilt, and communicate with clarity and compassion.

Amen.

LOVE, LUST, FOUNDATION

It started as a friendship.

Open conversations. Honest dialogue. We talked about past situations. Life lessons. Nothing hidden. Nothing rushed. And at the center of it all was God. That alignment mattered to me more than anything because by that point, I had been single for some time and had given my life to Christ. I was still learning what discipleship looked like. Still navigating sin. Still growing.

What I didn't expect was for that friendship to become something more.

Slowly. Naturally. Without pressure.

One thing that solidified the depth of this connection was the season we were in together. I was fasting for forty days during Lent, fighting daily battles, emotionally and spiritually. My grandmother, who was my best friend, passed away during that time. I was grieving, vulnerable, and trying to stay rooted. And even though we weren't officially dating or exclusive, he stayed supportive. Present. Grounding.

I remember asking him how he was holding up during that season, especially with the boundaries I was keeping. And he simply said he was there to support me.

That meant everything.

I had been used to relationships built on love bombing. On lust. On being pursued for how I looked or how I carried myself. This was different. Our conversations weren't about that. They were about growth. Purpose. Staying planted. Becoming better. The attraction was there, but it wasn't the foundation.

When we officially entered the relationship, something unexpected happened.

The chemistry didn't immediately show up the way it had in the past. We wanted closeness. We wanted affection. But it didn't come naturally at first. Not like the relationships that started with lust. We were best friends first. We prayed together. Talked about everything. Sat in silence comfortably. Watched sports. Did life.

But the physical expression of love felt... delayed.

It confused us. We even questioned whether we should go our separate ways because that spark didn't ignite instantly. But after a few days apart, we were drawn right back to each other.

That's when the lesson became clear.

Just because lust doesn't show up immediately doesn't mean the connection isn't real. Sometimes chemistry grows when the roots are deep. Sometimes God builds slowly so the foundation can last. What we have is intentional. Prayer-centered. Purpose-driven.

And we're still learning.

That relationship taught me that love doesn't always arrive loud. Sometimes it arrives steadily. Sometimes it whispers instead of burns. And when God is at the center, the connection doesn't have to rush; it has room to grow.

Scripture

"Love is patient, love is kind… it always protects, always trusts, always hopes, always perseveres."

— 1 Corinthians 13:4,7

Reflection Questions

- How do you distinguish between lust, love, and alignment in your relationships?
- Where might God be asking you to slow down instead of rushing into a connection?
- What does intentional love look like for you in this season?

Prayer

God, teach me to trust the connections You build slowly. Help me value alignment over intensity and patience over pressure. Keep my heart rooted in You as I grow in love, discernment, and purpose.

Amen.

GUARD YOUR EAR, PROTECT YOUR PEACE

One of the biggest lessons God has been teaching me is this: **guard your ear.**
Not just in relationships, in *life*.

Because the truth is, the loudest voices around you can become the loudest voices **inside** you.

Sometimes it's not even "bad people."
It's family.
It's friends.
It's coworkers.
It's the group chat.
It's opinions that mean well… but don't carry wisdom for *your* season.

And if you don't guard your ear, you'll start living your life based on what everyone else thinks you should do instead of what God already told you to do.

Boundaries aren't rude, they're holy.

Saying no to family doesn't mean you don't love them.
It means you're not available to be guilted, controlled, or drained.

Sometimes family will call you "funny acting" when you grow.
They'll say you're acting brand new.
They'll say you think you're better.
But really… they just miss the version of you that had no boundaries.

And God doesn't bless burnout.

Protecting rest is protection, not laziness.

Rest is not something you earn after you prove you're exhausted.
Rest is part of obedience.

If God needed rest, and He did, then so do you.

There are seasons where your "yes" is too expensive.
Where you don't need another plan, another event, another conversation, another obligation.
You need a nap.
You need quiet.
You need to breathe.

And you don't have to feel guilty for that.

Not over-explaining is emotional maturity.

Everybody doesn't deserve a full explanation.
Some people don't want clarity they want access.
They want to debate your boundary until you feel bad enough to drop it.

But you don't need a 10-minute speech to honor your peace.

Sometimes the boundary is simple:

- "I can't make it."
- "Not today."
- "I'm resting."
- "I'm not discussing that."
- "I'll get back to you when I'm ready."

Guarding your ear means guarding what you allow into your spirit because what you allow in will eventually come out in your attitude, your decisions, your joy, your confidence, and your faith.

You can't heal in the same noise that hurt you.
You can't grow while constantly defending your growth.

Grace doesn't mean you let people cross you.
Grace means you stay kind **without betraying yourself.**

Scripture

"Above all else, guard your heart, for everything you do flows from it."

— Proverbs 4:23

Reflection Questions

1. Where do I feel the most guilt when I try to set boundaries?
2. What area of my life needs a simple "no" so I can protect my peace?
3. Do I over-explain because I want to be understood or because I'm afraid to be disliked?

Prayer

God, help me guard my ear and protect my peace. Teach me to set boundaries without guilt and to rest without apology. Give me wisdom to know when to speak and when to be silent, and strength to honor what You're building in me, even when others don't understand it. In Jesus' name,

Amen.

WHEN LOVE REMAINS BUT ALIGNMENT CHANGES

Being away from your hometown and living in a bigger city teaches you a lot.

You meet people from different walks of life. You're exposed to new ideas, new conversations, new possibilities. And in the process, you learn more about yourself and about where you came from.

After being away for almost six years, going home for the holidays and for my mom's surgery was eye-opening. So much had happened while I was gone. I'd been in and out of relationships. I'd traveled. I'd grown spiritually. I'd worked new jobs, started businesses, and ended businesses. Life had stretched me.

While I stayed in touch with my friends from home through group chats and social media, we weren't deeply involved in each other's day-to-day lives anymore. So when we were finally all in the same space again, it was beautiful. The love was there. The laughter was there. The familiarity was there.

And so was the difference.

Some people had grown. Some people hadn't. And noticing that didn't come with judgment, it came with clarity.

I found myself asking hard but honest questions:

What does the next season of my life look like?

Who fits in it?

Who do I want around me when the blessings come?

If I get married, who would I want standing beside me?

If I open my home, who do I want in my space?

You'd think the answer would automatically be all your childhood friends. But sometimes love doesn't equal alignment.

I noticed behaviors, conversations, and choices that didn't reflect the life I'm working toward, especially as I continue walking with Christ. And that realization didn't come with anger or conflict. There were no harsh words. No falling out. Just awareness.

Some friendships had lasted over 25 years. And still, everybody can't come into every season.

That doesn't mean the love disappears. It doesn't mean the history is erased. It doesn't mean doors are slammed shut. It just means I'm being intentional with my space, my energy, and my growth.

You don't owe anyone access to your future just because they had access to your past.

Grace taught me this: it's okay to choose environments that help you grow. It's okay to outgrow conversations. And it's okay to love people from a distance while you move forward.

If anything, I hope my growth becomes light, not pressure. Influence, not judgment. And if paths cross again in alignment, I'll welcome it. But for now, I choose intentionality.

Scripture

"Do not be misled: 'Bad company corrupts good character.'"

— 1 Corinthians 15:33

Reflection Questions

- Who has been part of your past but may not fit your future?
- Where is God asking you to be more intentional with your space and energy?
- How can you honor history without sacrificing growth?

Prayer

God, thank You for the people who've walked with me through different seasons. Give me wisdom to discern who belongs in the next one, grace to love without guilt, and courage to protect the growth You're doing in me. Amen.

DON'T LOOK BACK

There's a version of freedom that feels like grief.

Because even when God is pulling you out of something…

part of you still misses what was familiar.

Not because it was good.

Not because it was safe.

But because it was known.

That's what Lot's wife teaches me.

God was rescuing them. He was literally pulling them out of destruction. And the instruction was simple:

Don't look back.

But she did.

And people always focus on the punishment, turning into a pillar of salt but what I can't stop thinking about is the moment before that.

What was she thinking when she turned around?

Was it regret?

Was it attachment?

Was it fear of the unknown?

Was it her mind replaying memories like, "At least I knew how to survive there…"?

Because sometimes we don't look back with our neck, we look back with our heart.

We go back to old relationships "just to check in."

We go back to old habits "just this once."

We go back to old mindsets when we're stressed.

We go back to old versions of ourselves when the new version feels uncomfortable.

And the craziest part?

You can be walking forward physically… while still living backward mentally.

That's why God didn't just say "leave."

He said don't look back.

Because looking back is how you start romanticizing what God delivered you from.

Looking back is how you start rewriting the story:

"It wasn't that bad…"

"Maybe I overreacted…"

"Maybe I should've stayed…"

"Maybe I can handle it now…"

No.

If God had to pull you out, it wasn't for you to turn around and stare at the fire.

Lot's wife represents the part of us that wants a miracle but still wants control.

The part of us that wants the new but keeps reaching for the old.

And what's heavy is this:

The delay isn't always the enemy. Sometimes the delay is your attachment.

God can open the door, but you can still be standing there looking behind you.

So today, I'm reminding myself:

If God said move, I don't need closure that looks like one more conversation.

If God said release, I don't need to explain myself again.

If God said new, I don't need to keep visiting old chapters like I live there.

Because the future requires forward focus.

And sometimes the reason you feel stuck is not because God stopped moving, it's because you keep looking back.

Scripture

"But Lot's wife looked back, and she became a pillar of salt."

-Genesis 19:26

Reflection

- What am I still looking at emotionally, mentally, or spiritually?
- What has God already delivered me from that I keep romanticizing?
- What would it look like if I moved forward without checking behind?

Prayer

God, help me obey even when my emotions want to rewind.

Strengthen me to release what You removed.

Heal the part of me that misses what was familiar, even if it was harmful.

Give me forward faith, forward focus, and the courage to keep walking.

In Jesus' name, amen.

SECTION 5: GOD IN THE DETAILS

MIRACLES ALL AROUND

Could you imagine walking with Jesus… watching miracle after miracle happen right in front of you?

Blind eyes opened.
Bodies healed.
Lives restored.
People crying tears of relief because God showed up for them in real time.

Now imagine you're faithful. You're serving. You're doing the work. You've built your life around following God. And then when it's time for *your* miracle… you experience loss.

A miscarriage.
Infertility.
The kind of disappointment that makes you whisper, "God… why me?"
The kind of heartbreak that doesn't just hurt your body it tests your belief.

That's what people don't always talk about: how hard it is to keep your faith when you're watching God bless everyone else and your arms are still empty.

And I won't pretend that's easy.
Because it's not.

But what I do know is this: God doesn't waste pain. And He doesn't place you in trials to destroy you. He allows certain battles to develop you. To deepen your roots. To strengthen your faith when it's not convenient.

I think about the woman who touched the edge of Jesus' cloak. She didn't need a full conversation. She didn't need to be called out. She didn't need permission. She just believed: *If I can touch Him… I'll be healed.*

That kind of faith doesn't come from comfort.
It comes from desperation.

From endurance.
From suffering that refuses to let go of hope.

If you're struggling with infertility…
If you've experienced miscarriage…
If you're carrying grief that people can't see…
I want you to know you are not forgotten. You are not being punished.
And you are not less of a woman because your journey looks different.

Yes, doctors matter. Community matters. Wise counsel matters.
But above all: your faith matters.

Because even when you don't understand God's timing, you can still trust His heart.

And sometimes the miracle isn't just the outcome it's the strength God builds in you while you wait.

Scripture

"She said, 'If I only touch his cloak, I will be healed.'"

— Matthew 9:21

Reflection Questions

- Where am I struggling to trust God because I don't understand His timing?
- What would "faith in the waiting" look like for me this week?
- Who can I safely talk to about this without shame or pressure?

Prayer

God, I'm trying to trust You in the middle of disappointment. When my heart is heavy, and my questions feel louder than my faith, hold me close. Strengthen me in the waiting. Heal what has been lost in my body, my mind, and my spirit. Help me believe You are still good, still present, and still writing my story with love. In Jesus' name, Amen.

WHEN YOU DON'T HAVE TO PROVE IT

If you paid attention to football or the NFL draft in 2025, you saw what happened with Shadeur Sanders.

He got pushed back.

He got questioned.

And people started running with narratives about his "attitude" and his "arrogance."

Which is wild because if anyone had a reason to be confident, it was him.

He was raised by an NFL legend.

He was trained by one of the greatest.

He showed up prepared.

But what really changed people's perspective wasn't his talent; it was how he carried himself under pressure.

People tried to provoke him.

They tried to rage-bait him into saying something slick about coaches or the system.

They tried to make him react.

And he didn't.

He stayed smooth.

He stayed respectful.

He stayed grounded.

That's when you realize something powerful:

True confidence doesn't need to be loud.

Anybody can pop off when they feel disrespected.

Anybody can flex when they feel underestimated.

But real strength is staying humble when you don't have to be.

That's "when they go low, we go high" energy.

That's letting your character speak louder than your ego.

Because when you know who you are,

You don't need to convince anyone else.

Scripture

"The Lord will fight for you; you need only to be still."

— Exodus 14:14

Reflection

- Where in your life do you feel tempted to prove yourself?
- How do you usually respond when people misunderstand you?
- What would change if you let your consistency speak instead of your reactions?

Prayer

God, help me to be confident without being combative.

Teach me how to stay grounded when I'm misunderstood.

Let my character speak louder than my emotions.

Give me the strength to stay humble, even when I know who I am.

In Jesus' name,

Amen.

WHEN I LET THE INTERNET TELL ME I NEEDED MORE

I always thought I had a cute shape. Flat stomach. Defined abs. Athletic build. I was confident in my body until I got on social media.

Scrolling through Instagram, I started seeing all these influencers with exaggerated curves. Big hips. Tiny waists. Bodies that looked like the new standard. I turned thirty, and suddenly what once felt like enough didn't anymore. I still liked how I looked, but I wanted what I was seeing. I wanted those hips. I wanted more curves. I felt like I was missing something.

And when you finally have the means to change what you don't feel comfortable with, the temptation is strong.

So I went and got surgery.

What's crazy is the surgeon looked at me like I was out of my mind. He said, "You don't even have fat to take." And instead of seeing that as a sign, I did the opposite. I tried to intentionally gain weight so there would be something to remove and transfer. I was trying to become something I wasn't meant to be.

After the surgery, I realized something painful: I still didn't look like what I saw online. And later after moving to Atlanta I learned why. Many of the women I compared myself to weren't one-and-done. They were getting multiple surgeries. Injections. Enhancements. Touch-ups. Things no one talks about online.

I altered my body chasing an image that wasn't real.

What hurts the most is that I was already blessed. I had a body people worked hard for. A six-pack. Strength. Health. And I let comparison convince me it wasn't enough. Ironically, as I grew older into my mid-thirties, my body naturally developed in ways I once tried to force. Time did what surgery couldn't.

If I could talk to my younger self, I'd tell her this: Be patient. Your body will grow with you. You are beautiful already. You don't need to reshape yourself to match something filtered, edited, and often fake.

Grace taught me that comparison is loud, but truth is steady. And learning to love yourself takes time, but it's worth the wait.

Scripture

"I praise You because I am fearfully and wonderfully made."

— Psalm 139:14

Reflection Questions

- Where has comparison made you question what was once enough?
- What messages about beauty have shaped your self-image?
- How can patience and gratitude change the way you view yourself today?

Prayer

God, forgive me for the times I questioned Your workmanship. Help me see myself through Your eyes, not through comparison or pressure. Teach me patience with myself and gratitude for the body You gave me.

Amen.

WHEN THE ENEMY MAKES YOU QUESTION YOUR IDENTITY

One thing Satan does very well is make you question who you are.

He attacks identity first because if you don't know who you are, you'll start believing lies about what you deserve. He makes you forget that you're worthy of everything God has for you, regardless of your past, your mistakes, or the relationships that didn't work out.

If you desire to be a wife, you're worthy of that.

If you want to be a mother, you're worthy of that.

If you want abundance, peace, love, travel, stability, you're worthy of that.

Your past does not disqualify you.

But the enemy will try to convince you otherwise.

He'll use comparison. Social media. Timelines. Highlight reels. He'll make you look at other people's lives and think you're behind, not enough, or out of place. He'll whisper, "Look where they are and look where you aren't."

I've felt that before.

I remember dating someone who moved in circles with influencers, actors, and people with big platforms. And it made me question myself. I thought, What do you want with me? I'm just a regular girl. I don't chase attention. I have a private page. I don't like being seen like that.

And maybe, on paper, I wasn't "the type."

But what we built was a friendship rooted in depth, honesty, and connection. One of the strongest friendships I've ever had. And it had nothing to do with how I looked or what I had; it had everything to do with my heart.

That taught me something important.

God doesn't measure you the way the world does.

Comparison is the enemy's favorite distraction because it pulls your focus off God's timing and places it on someone else's assignment. And when you compare, you forget that you are exactly where God wants you to be.

Not late.

Not behind.

Not forgotten.

Just becoming.

Grace taught me this: the moment you stop comparing, you start walking confidently in your purpose. Satan wants you to believe you're lacking, but God is reminding you that you're chosen.

Trust His timing.

Trust His purpose.

And trust that what He has for you will not miss you.

Scripture

"For we are God's handiwork, created in Christ Jesus to do good works."

— Ephesians 2:10

Reflection Questions

- Where has comparison made you question your worth?
- What lies have you believed about what you deserve?
- How can you shift your focus back to God's timing for your life?

Prayer

God, help me silence the lies that question my worth and identity. Remind me who I am in You and teach me to trust Your timing over comparison. Strengthen my confidence in the purpose You've placed on my life.

Amen.

THE VERSION GOD SEES

What version of me does God see?

Does he see the little girl with the candy store?

hustling, counting coins, learning how to survive?

Does he see the teenage girl

laughing too loud, dancing with her friends, free and careless?

Does he see the young mother?

loving fiercely, choosing the wrong men, trying to fill emotional gaps with material things?

Does he see the woman in her 30s

in a new city, questioning her worth, comparing herself to everyone around her?

Or does He see who I am now?

the woman learning how to forgive without needing an apology,

to give without needing applause,

to love without losing herself?

I think God sees it all.

Not the broken pieces

the becoming.

We spend so much of our lives trying to become impressive to people.

We chase relationships.

We try to look successful, attractive, wanted.

But none of that matters if our spirit is out of alignment.

This year, my goal isn't to look good.

It's to be right.

Not in the eyes of social media.

Not in the eyes of my job.

Not even in the eyes of someone I love.

In the eyes of God.

Because when God is proud of who you are becoming,

Everything else lines up naturally.

Love finds you.

Peace finds you.

Provision finds you.

Not because you chased it

but because you became the version of yourself that could receive it.

Scripture

"For those God foreknew he also predestined to be conformed to the image of his Son..."

—Romans 8:29

Reflection

- What version of myself have I been trying to impress people with?
- What version of me do I believe God is calling me to grow into?
- What habits, thoughts, or relationships no longer match who I'm becoming?

Prayer

God, help me become the version of myself that brings You joy.

Strip away the need for validation and replace it with alignment.

Let who I am in private match who I claim to be in public.

I want to be someone you're proud of.

Amen.

GODS FAVORITE

Let the way you speak about your life sound so bold that it almost feels unreal.

We already do this for the people we love.

We tell our children, "You're smart. You're beautiful. You can do anything."

We tell our partners, "You're amazing. You're handsome. You're special."

But then, when it comes to ourselves, we get quiet.

No, speak to yourself with the same love, confidence, and belief.

I tell myself all the time:

I'm blessed.

I'm anointed.

I'm protected.

I'm loved.

I'm wealthy.

I'm healthy.

I'm happy.

And my favorite one…

I'm God's favorite.

Yes, I know He has millions and millions of children, but I'm still His favorite.

Why?

Because I woke up today.

Because there is breath in my lungs.

Because grace found me again this morning.

Because God keeps making a way for me when I shouldn't even have one.

That's favor.

That's anointing.

There was a TikTok trend in which one grandchild wore a "Grandma's Favorite" shirt at Christmas. They pretended she gifted it to them and surprised their grandmother. Everybody would start laughing and arguing about who was really her favorite because everyone wants to be chosen.

That's how I feel about God.

Not because He gives me more than others,

but because I believe He sees me.

He hears me.

He covers me.

He walks with me.

When you start speaking over your life with that kind of confidence,

You challenge everything sent to destroy you.

Fear can't live where faith speaks loudly.

Doubt can't survive where identity is clear.

Say it:

I'm God's favorite.

And He always looks out for me.

Scripture

"For the mouth speaks what the heart is full of."

— Luke 6:45

Reflection

- How do I usually speak about myself kindly or critically?
- What would change if I spoke over my life with confidence instead of fear?
- What blessings do I already have that prove God's favor in my life?

Prayer

God, help me see myself the way You see me.

Teach me to speak life instead of doubt.

Let my words reflect my faith and not my fear.

Thank you for choosing me, covering me, and loving me.

Amen.

FRESH START

Have you ever had one of those mornings?

You ate something you shouldn't have the night before, and your stomach is fighting you all night.

Your acid reflux is acting up.

You had wild dreams.

Your sleep was trash.

Then you wake up, and your kids aren't cooperating.

They missed the bus.

Now you're driving them.

You spill something.

You forgot something.

Your phone is ringing.

Your job wants you early.

And just to top it all off…

Your barista made your coffee wrong.

It's enough to make you say, "NOW LORD, YOU KNOW WHAT."

And the truth is, most days don't go bad because of one big thing.

They go bad because of how we let the small things stack.

I try to wake up early.

I try to do my devotionals.

I try to listen to affirmations.

I try to move slowly and intentionally.

But life doesn't always allow that.

So I had to learn how to reset in real time.

That's where my gratitude walks come in.

That's where gospel music comes in.

That's where sitting in my car for two minutes before walking into work comes in.

Because sometimes you don't need an hour, you need a moment.

A moment to breathe.

A moment to say, "God, help me not let this morning ruin my day."

The energy you carry spills onto everyone you touch.

Your kids feel it.

Your coworkers feel it.

Your partner feels it.

So if you don't shift it, it spreads.

You don't have to fake being happy, but you do have to choose not to stay stuck.

Even if you're late.

Even if things are messy.

Even if your coffee is wrong.

Pause.

Breathe.

Reset.

You still get to decide how this day goes.

Scripture

"I will give you a new heart and put a new spirit in you"

— Ezekiel 36:26

Reflection

- What usually throws off my mornings?
- How can I create a two-minute reset when things go wrong?
- What small habit could help me start again instead of spiraling?

Prayer

God, help me reset when life feels rushed.

Help me breathe when things feel heavy.

Let me move through this day with peace, not pressure.

Amen.

KNOWING WHEN TO ASK FOR HELP

If you know, you know.

Growing up before the 2000s, therapy wasn't even a thought. Mental health wasn't a conversation. You dealt with things. You pushed through. You prayed. You kept moving.

Mental health didn't really enter my world until COVID.

Something shifted during that time. Maybe it was the isolation. Maybe it was fear. Maybe it was the constant uncertainty: Are people sick? Are they safe? Why are they wearing masks? Why aren't they? Everything felt heightened. And I think for a lot of people, something quietly snapped.

Around 2023, I noticed something was off with me.

I started having random crying spells. Moments of sudden sadness that didn't make sense. And that concerned me because I'm not overly emotional. I've learned how to manage my emotions well. So when those moments kept happening, I knew I needed to talk to someone.

Not just anyone.

I wanted someone who looked like me. Someone around my age. Someone who might understand my background. I didn't want a forced conversation or someone just saying, "Tell me more." I wanted understanding without explanation.

So I found a therapist.

And it helped.

She didn't replace God; she supported my walk with Him. She encouraged my faith, my church involvement, and my journey toward baptism. And at the same time, she became a neutral space. Someone who didn't know my family. Didn't know my friends. Didn't have a bias toward my partner or my past.

Just a safe place to process.

That doesn't mean God stopped being my first call. He's still my main source. Always. But I learned something important: it's okay to recognize when you need help.

Sometimes you don't want to call your friends because they might give you the wrong advice.

Sometimes your mom, your siblings, and your partner mean well, but their perspective is clouded by emotion.

Sometimes you just need an unbiased ear.

And that's okay.

Asking for help doesn't mean you lack faith. It means you're self-aware. It means you're choosing healing over silence. It means you understand that God works through people too.

Grace taught me this: you can pray and go to therapy. You can trust God and talk things through. One doesn't cancel out the other.

Just make sure the help you seek aligns with your values and never replaces your relationship with God.

Scripture

"Plans are established by seeking advice; so if you wage war obtain guidance."

— Proverbs 20:18

Reflection Questions

- How were you taught to handle emotions growing up?
- Where might God be inviting you to seek support instead of silence?
- What boundaries help you protect both your faith and your mental health?

Prayer

God, thank You for being my constant source of strength. Give me wisdom to know when I need support and humility to ask for it. Help me care for my mind and spirit while staying rooted in You.

Amen.

THERE'S NO WRONG WAY TO PRAY

"Our Father, who art in heaven…"

That's how many of us were taught to pray. The words. The order. The flow. And for a long time, I believed that if I didn't pray that way, God wouldn't listen. That my words had to sound right. That I had to be in a church. That I had to get it perfect for it to count.

I thought prayer was scripted.

Before my journey, I truly believed that if I didn't say the right words or say them the right way, God might not hear me. Or worse, He might not care. And then something clicked.

My relationship with God is my relationship with God.

It's personal. It's intimate. And it's not rehearsed.

Sometimes I talk to God the same way I talk to my friends. Or my mom. Or my partner. Sometimes I ask questions. Sometimes I vent. Sometimes I laugh. Sometimes I cry. And sometimes I just sit in silence because He already knows.

There is no blueprint for intimacy with God.

How I pray isn't always polished. It didn't start out "holy." I've had to catch myself from swearing. I've had to remind myself not to call God "bro" out of frustration. But here's the truth: God isn't intimidated by my humanity.

He's my Father.

And like any real relationship, communication grows over time. You don't become a prayer warrior overnight. You don't wake up speaking in tongues and pacing the pews. You start where you are.

"God, what's up?"

"God, thank You."

"God, I don't understand this."

"God, thank You for keeping me today."

"God… good looking out."

Simple. Honest. Real.

Prayer doesn't always have to be a request. Sometimes it's gratitude. Sometimes it's acknowledgment. Sometimes it's just showing up.

Grace taught me this: God would rather hear your imperfect words than your silence. He meets you where you are, not where you think you should be.

So don't be afraid to start. Don't be afraid to talk. Don't be afraid to be real.

You have to start somewhere.

Scripture

"The Lord is near to all who call on Him in truth."

— Psalm 145:18

Reflection Questions

- What fears or beliefs have shaped how you pray?
- How might prayer feel different if you removed the pressure to perform and focused on honesty?
- What would it look like to simply talk to God today?

Prayer

God, thank You for meeting me where I am. Help me release fear and embrace honesty when I come to You. Teach me that intimacy grows with time, trust, and truth.

Amen.

CHOOSING GRACE OVER CRASHING OUT

I've been seeing posts lately that say things like, "Two minutes cost me 28 years," or "Five seconds changed my life forever." Stories about people who made one split-second decision and lost everything.

That thought stays with me.

Because sometimes destruction doesn't come from long-term choices. Sometimes it comes from a moment. A reaction. A refusal to pause.

We were in Durham, North Carolina, headed to a small holistic shop to grab detox teas and natural products. Quiet day. Good energy. Nothing out of the ordinary. The kind of day where everything feels aligned.

We parked behind the building in an open lot with plenty of space. Inside, the young woman working the counter was explaining the benefits of the teas, weighing them, and bagging them. Calm. Peaceful.

Then an older man stormed in.

Aggressive. Loud. Demanding to know whose car was parked outside. When we said it was ours, he told us to move it immediately. The worker explained we were finishing up and would be right out.

That wasn't good enough.

Less than a minute later, he came back, this time inviting my partner outside. Not asking. Demanding. Wanting to pull him away from me. Away from witnesses. Into a space with no cameras.

And that's when my spirit checked in.

This wasn't about parking.

This man was battling something we knew nothing about. And we had just become the outlet for it.

My partner, six-four, 240 pounds, had every ability to defend himself. And the older man had no idea who he was dealing with, what was in our car, or what that confrontation could turn into. In a split second, someone could've been hurt. Someone could've gone to jail. Someone's life could've been changed forever.

So we chose grace.

We moved the car. We walked away. Not because we were wrong but because peace was more important than pride.

Later, we learned the man owned the lot and had an ongoing issue with the shop's customers. We were just the unlucky ones who showed up that day.

And that's the lesson.

Sometimes people aren't angry at you. They're angry at life. At a loss. At disappointment. At things you'll never know about. And engaging them in their storm can pull you into consequences that were never meant for you.

Grace isn't a weakness.

Grace is discernment.

Grace is restraint.

Grace is choosing freedom over ego.

God covered us both that day. He covered my partner by softening his response. And He covered that man by keeping him from provoking the wrong person at the wrong time.

Walking away saved more than an argument; it protected futures.

Scripture

"A gentle answer turns away wrath, but a harsh word stirs up anger."

— Proverbs 15:1

Reflection Questions

- How do you usually respond when someone disrespects you unexpectedly?
- Have you ever realized later that walking away protected you from something bigger?
- What does giving grace look like in moments that challenge your pride?

Prayer

God, help me pause before reacting. Give me wisdom to know when to speak and when to walk away. Protect me from moments that could cost me more than they're worth, and help me choose grace even when it's hard.

Amen.

SECTION 6: HARD LESSONS, SOFT HEART

A HARD HEAD MAKES A SOFT BUTT

How many of us grew up hearing the old saying, "A hard head makes a soft butt"? Back then it just sounded like something our parents said to get us to listen. But as adults… whew. That phrase hits different.

What it really means is this: when you don't listen to your intuition, to your discernment, to the quiet nudges God places in your spirit, you end up learning the hard way.

God is always whispering before He has to shout.

He sends signs before He sends storms.

He gives you a feeling before He gives you a consequence.

But when we ignore that still small voice because we want what we want, when we want it, we often walk ourselves straight into unnecessary pain. We stay in situations we already feel uneasy about. We entertain people we were warned about. We push forward even when something in our spirit is telling us to pause.

And then, when things fall apart, we ask God why when deep down, we already knew.

A hard head will always lead to a softer landing… and not in a good way.

The beautiful part is that God still gives grace, even when we don't listen. But growth looks like learning to hear Him sooner, so we don't have to be broken to be redirected.

Scripture

"Whoever remains stiff-necked after many rebukes will suddenly be destroyed without remedy."

- Proverbs 29:1

Reflection Questions

- What has God been trying to tell me that I've been ignoring?
- Where in my life have I felt uneasy, but pushed forward anyway?
- Am I trusting my discernment, or am I constantly overriding it?
- What would change if I listened the first time?

Prayer

God, thank You for always speaking to me, even when I don't always listen. Help me to recognize Your voice more clearly. Give me the courage to pause when You tell me to pause, and the wisdom to move when You tell me to move. Forgive me for the times I chose stubbornness over surrender. Teach me how to trust You before I have to learn the hard way. I don't want to be redirected through pain —I want to be led through obedience.

In Jesus' name, Amen.

TRUSTING GOD IN THE SIMPLE SEASONS

When I think about the most straightforward instructions God gave us, the ones written plainly and handed down to Moses, they weren't complicated.

Don't put anything before Me.

Don't create idols.

Don't covet what others have.

At their core, these commandments are about trust.

We don't always recognize coveting for what it is.

Sometimes it doesn't look like jealousy; it looks like impatience.

It looks like dissatisfaction.

It looks like saying, "God, this isn't enough."

It may be a season of peanut butter and jelly.

A season of ramen noodles.

A season of stretching meals, stretching faith, stretching patience.

And for some people, even that is a blessing.

But comparison creeps in quietly.

Why can't I have what they have?

Why am I not eating steak when everyone else seems to be dining well?

Why does it feel like I'm always in a waiting season?

Coveting doesn't always mean wanting someone else's exact life; it means refusing to rest in the one God has currently given you.

God never promised luxury in every season.

But He did promise provision.

And provision isn't always material; it's spiritual.

Sometimes God feeds you peace instead of plenty.

Sometimes He gives you rest instead of excess.

Sometimes He teaches you gratitude before He teaches you abundance.

A filet mignon season may come, but this might be the season where God is teaching you how to trust Him with the basics.

And when you learn to honor God in the simple seasons, you'll be prepared to steward the greater ones.

Scripture

"Keep your lives free from the love of money and be content with what you have, because God has said, 'Never will I leave you; never will I forsake you.'"

— Hebrews 13:5

Reflection Questions

- Where have you struggled with contentment in this season?
- Are there areas where comparison has replaced gratitude?
- What has God already provided that you may be overlooking?

Prayer

God, help me trust You even when provision looks simple. Teach me to rest in what You've given me today and not long for what isn't meant for me yet. I know You will provide spiritually and emotionally, in Your perfect timing.

Amen.

FAITH THAT KEEPS YOU AFLOAT

One of the most powerful stories in the Bible about faith versus fear is the account of Peter walking on water.

Imagine it.

You're in the middle of a storm.

The waves are crashing.

The wind is loud.

And Jesus tells you to come.

And somehow by faith you step off the boat.

You're walking on water.

Doing the impossible.

Defying logic.

Moving purely on trust and obedience.

But then something happens.

You start paying attention to the storm.

The noise.

The waves.

The "this shouldn't be possible" thoughts.

Fear creeps in.

And the moment Peter looks away from Jesus, he sinks.

That's the part that hits me every time.

Because it wasn't the storm that made him sink.

It wasn't the waves.

It wasn't the wind.

It was distraction.

The second Peter took his eyes off God and focused on what could go wrong instead of what God already told him would happen, he began to sink.

And how often do we do the same?

God calls us to step out.

To trust Him.

To believe in more.

And for a moment, we're walking on water.

Then the noise gets loud.

Bills. Opinions. Social media. Fear. Doubt. Comparison.

"What if this doesn't work?"

"What if I fail?"

"What if I look foolish?"

And suddenly, we're sinking.

But here's where grace steps in.

Peter didn't pretend he wasn't sinking.

He didn't try to save himself.

He reached out and said, "Lord, save me."

And Jesus did.

Even after Peter lost focus.

Even after fear interrupted faith.

Jesus still saved him.

Then He asked him a question not to shame him, but to teach him:

Why did you doubt?

Grace doesn't mean you won't stumble.

Grace means God will still reach for you when you do.

Don't let outside noise distract you from what God is making possible.

Don't let fear convince you that the impossible can't happen.

If God told you to step out, He already accounted for the storm.

Keep your eyes on Him.

Faith keeps you afloat.

Scripture

"But when he saw the wind, he was afraid and, beginning to sink, cried out, 'Lord, save me!' Immediately Jesus reached out his hand and caught him."

— Matthew 14:30–31

Reflection Questions

- What distractions have pulled your focus away from God's calling?
- Where has fear caused you to hesitate or sink?
- How can you refocus your faith in this season?

Prayer

God, help me keep my eyes on You when fear tries to take over. Remind me that You are bigger than the storm and faithful even when I lose focus. Strengthen my faith and catch me when I stumble.

Amen.

FASTING WITH INTENTION

I've always fasted even before I took my walk and got baptized.

When I was younger, fasting looked simple. I'd give up candy. Soda. TV. Something I liked, but something I could survive without. It felt more like a challenge or even a diet than a spiritual discipline.

As I got older, fasting changed.

It became deeper. More intentional. I stopped eating while the sun was up. I removed certain foods. I removed distractions. And eventually, it stopped being about what I was giving up and became about who I was surrendering to.

Fasting required more than convenience; it required denial.

It wasn't just about food. It was about denying my flesh. My habits. My impulses. My need to be seen or understood. I fasted privately. Quietly. No announcements. No explanations. People didn't know what I was carrying inside because I couldn't talk about it, which made it harder.

But it also made it holy.

I remember when our church did a 72-hour fast, nothing but water. It was brutal. But it drew me closer to God in a way nothing else had. That experience changed how I approached my 40-day fast. I didn't want something surface-level. I wanted closeness. I wanted clarity. I wanted to deny everything that could pull me backward so I could move forward anchored in Him.

This time, fasting wasn't transactional.

I wasn't bargaining with God. I wasn't asking for things just to receive. I was writing things down daily. Asking for guidance. Asking for clarity. Asking to be aligned with the next season of my life. Asking God to help me not return to places I'd outgrown.

And I learned something important: fasting doesn't force God's hand, it softens your heart.

It tunes your spirit to hear Him more clearly. It quiets the noise. It teaches discipline. And it reminds you that growth requires sacrifice real sacrifice.

Grace taught me this: fasting isn't about perfection or punishment. It's about intention. And when your intention is to draw closer to God, He honors that every time.

Scripture

"Draw near to God, and He will draw near to you."

— James 4:8

Reflection Questions

- How has your understanding of sacrifice evolved over time?
- What distractions might God be asking you to lay down in this season?
- Are your prayers focused on outcomes or alignment?

Prayer

God, help me fast with intention, not routine. Teach me how to deny my flesh so my spirit can grow stronger. Draw me closer to You, refine my desires, and guide me into the season You're preparing me for.

Amen.

ONLINE, BUT STILL ALL IN

There's this idea that if you're not sitting in a pew every Sunday, you're somehow not really walking with God.

That's just not true anymore.

We live in a world where life comes fast.

Jobs don't protect Sundays.

Kids have schedules.

Commutes are long.

Burnout is real.

And some people are still healing from what COVID did to their nervous systems.

So sometimes, being an online Christian is all you can do, and God still meets you right there.

I physically go to church, but I also get poured into by pastors all across the country.

I listen to Pastor Keon Henderson in Houston.

I listen to Pastor Mike Jr. in Alabama.

I listen to Pastor Philip Anthony Mitchell in Atlanta.

Depending on the season, I'll tune into Sarah Jakes too.

Different voices.

Different styles.

Same God.

And what I love about this generation of faith is that you can still be a real steward even from your couch.

Every service has a QR code.

Every ministry gives you a way to sow.

And I've learned something powerful about giving:

You don't give to get.

You give because you're grateful.

I now set aside a portion of my income automatically for giving, even in seasons when I don't have much. I don't even see it. It goes straight into my giving account, because I want my heart to stay in alignment with God's.

Our money isn't really ours anyway.

It's meant to flow, not just sit.

And yes… sometimes church for me looks like:

Sitting in my room.

Worship music playing.

Me clapping by myself.

Dancing.

Tapping the air when the pastor says, "tap your neighbor."

Because spiritually?

I'm not alone.

I'm connected.

Online church doesn't mean offline faith.

It means you're showing up however you can.

And God honors that.

Scripture

"For where two or three are gathered in my name, there am I among them."

— Matthew 18:20

(Even if one of them is on Wi-Fi.)

Reflection

- Where do I feel spiritually fed right now?
- Am I giving with gratitude or expectation?
- How can I stay consistent in my faith even when life is busy?

Prayer

God, thank You for meeting me wherever I am.

In my car.

In my room.

On my phone.

Help me give with a grateful heart and stay rooted no matter how I worship.

Amen.

POWER OF THE TONGUE

My friend Dave has been helping me work on the power of the tongue, being intentional with my words, and choosing to speak life and positivity, even when everything around me feels heavy.

One way I practice this is through what I call gratitude walks.

When I'm at work, and things are getting tough, managers are frustrating me, pressure is building, and I feel overlooked, instead of lashing out or letting my thoughts spiral, I pause. I step away. I take a walk around the building. And I thank God.

Not for the problems but for the blessings.

I stop myself from complaining about what's going wrong and intentionally focus on what's going right. I thank God for the roof over my head. For food in my refrigerator. For Wi-Fi. For my car. For my health. For my mom's health. For my son. For being kept another day.

Sometimes the gratitude is big. Sometimes it's small. But it's always intentional.

Instead of replaying what my manager said, or stressing about my son's behavior at school, or worrying about what I can't control, I shift my focus. I speak of the good. I speak about what I intend to go well. And slowly, my spirit follows my words.

That practice has changed everything for me.

It reframed my mindset from a glass half-empty to a glass half-full. It taught me that gratitude isn't denial; it's discipline. I'm not pretending problems don't exist. I'm choosing not to let them dominate my spirit.

And I've learned something important: when I speak life, I give myself grace and honor God. I acknowledge what He's already done rather than just asking for more. And gratitude creates room for blessing. Life doesn't always get easier. But my response gets healthier.

Scripture

"The tongue has the power of life and death, and those who love it will eat its fruit"

— Proverbs 18:21

Reflection Questions

- What do you speak most often about when you're overwhelmed, complaint, or gratitude?
- How might your mindset shift if you practiced gratitude daily?
- What small blessings have you overlooked in the middle of stress?

Prayer

God, teach me to speak life even when circumstances feel heavy. Help me pause before reacting, choose gratitude over complaint, and trust that You are working even when I can't see it yet.

Amen.

ALIGNMENT VS. OPPORTUNITY

One of the most overlooked prayers is the prayer for discernment.

We pray for doors to open.

We pray for blessings.

We pray for elevation.

But not every open door is in alignment.

Some doors open to test you.

Some doors open to distract you.

Some doors open to see if you'll settle.

That's how people end up in jobs that drain them, relationships that confuse them, and situations that look good on paper but break them on the inside. We assume that because something is available, it must be God, but sometimes it's just accessible.

Money can look good.

The commute can look good.

The title can look good.

The attention can feel good.

But if it pulls you away from who you're becoming, it's not aligned.

Discernment is what tells you:

"This is for me."

"This is not for me."

"This looks good, but it will cost me more than it gives."

And sometimes the blessing isn't the opportunity

It's the clarity to walk away.

Scripture

"In their hearts humans plan their course, but the Lord establishes their steps."

— Proverbs 16:9

Reflection

- Have you ever said yes to something that felt off but looked good?
- What signs do you ignore when something isn't aligned?
- Where do you need discernment right now?

Prayer

God, I thank You for every door You open.

And every door You close.

Give me the discernment to distinguish between opportunity and alignment.

Protect me from stepping into things that look good but aren't good for me.

Guide my decisions, so I move with purpose, not desperation.

In Jesus' name, Amen.

DELUSIONAL FAITH

I was watching a sermon by Pastor Mike Jr. on YouTube, and one thing he said stopped me in my tracks.

He said, " Sometimes your faith has to look delusional.

Not reckless.

Not irresponsible.

But bold.

He said you have to believe in God so deeply that you start preparing for what hasn't happened yet. You start looking for the house before you have the money. You start speaking about the promotion before you get the offer. You start making room for the blessing before it arrives.

Because your God is a big God.

And that word hit me.

I'm a few months away from my lease being up, and after hearing that message, something shifted in me. I didn't just think about where I am, I started thinking about where I'm going.

I want a townhouse for my son and me.

Not a mansion. Not anything flashy.

Just something rooted. Something peaceful. Something that feels like the next chapter.

Where I live, townhouses cost millions.

But instead of scrolling Zillow in fear, I started scrolling it in faith.

I went from the rent section to the buy section.

Not because the money is sitting there right now, but because the vision is.

Because if God placed it in my heart, He also has a way to bring it to pass.

And I know how it sounds.

People will call it unrealistic.

People will call it crazy.

People will say I should be more practical.

But faith has never been about playing it safe.

Faith is about believing that God can move you in one season what would take others ten.

Faith is trusting that when He gives you a vision, He already built the path.

So yes, I'm looking at homes.

I'm dreaming.

I'm preparing.

I'm moving as if God is about to do what He said He would. And I refuse to apologize for believing Him.

Scripture

"Now to Him who is able to do exceedingly, abundantly above all that we ask or think..."

— Ephesians 3:20

Reflection Questions

- What has God placed on my heart that feels bigger than my current reality?
- Where am I still limiting God with fear?
- What would it look like to prepare for the blessing before it arrives?

Prayer

God, help me believe You at Your word. Give me bold faith to prepare for what You are about to do. Let my hope be louder than my doubt.

Amen.

UNIQUELY POSITIONED

I know God is working on me because lately I find messages in everything.

Movies.

Music.

Conversations.

Even moments that are meant to be entertaining end up speaking directly to my spirit.

I recently watched a movie called Marty Supreme, and as funny, chaotic, and intense as it was, one line stopped me in my tracks.

He said: "I'm uniquely positioned."

The movie follows a man whose skill was something most people would overlook: table tennis. Ping pong. Something people wouldn't normally associate with greatness or destiny unless you're Forest Gump. But he believed in himself so deeply that nothing could convince him otherwise.

Not ridicule.

Not obstacles.

Not the odds.

He believed that this the thing that felt small to others was his calling. And because he believed it, he pursued it relentlessly.

That phrase stuck with me because it reminded me of something God has been teaching me:

We are each uniquely positioned for a reason.

Not randomly placed.

Not delayed.

Not behind.

Positioned.

Where I am in life right now isn't an accident. The experiences I've had, the setbacks I've endured, the skills I've picked up along the way, none of it is wasted. God placed me here with intention.

Sometimes we downplay our gifts because they don't look impressive to the world. Sometimes we hesitate because our calling doesn't follow a traditional path. But God doesn't measure purpose the way people do.

What matters is belief.

Consistency.

Faith.

If God placed something in your heart, no matter how unconventional, He also equipped you to pursue it.

You don't have to look like anyone else.

You don't have to follow their timeline.

You don't have to prove yourself to the world.

You just have to stay obedient to what God placed inside you. Because you, too, are uniquely positioned.

Scripture

"And who knows but that you have come to your royal position for such a time as this?"

— Esther 4:14

Reflection Questions

- What gifts or passions have I minimized because they seemed small?
- Where do I believe God has positioned me right now?
- Am I trusting His placement, or am I fighting it?

Prayer

God, help me trust where You have placed me. Give me confidence in the gifts You've given me, even when they don't look impressive to others. Help me walk boldly in my purpose, knowing You don't make mistakes.

Amen.

DARK ENOUGH TO HEAR

When I visited Rock City Church in Birmingham, I met a woman named Quon.

She had been a member since 2010, back when Pastor Mike was just starting out in his twenties. That alone told me something. People don't stay somewhere that long unless something real is happening there.

She told me a story I'll never forget.

At the time, she was attending a more traditional church. But her son had found Pastor Mike's church, and he was on fire for God. He kept asking her to come. Eventually, she agreed not because she wanted to go, but because she wanted to understand why her son was so moved.

When they walked up to the doors, her son grabbed her hand and said,

"Hold my hand… It's dark in there."

That scared her.

Dark church?

What kind of place was this?

And right when they sat down, Pastor Mike said something that changed everything for her.

He said people always complained that it was dark, but who said prayer had to happen in a bright room?

When it's dark, you stop looking at everybody else.

You stop worrying about who's watching.

You stop performing.

You just… pray.

That was the moment she understood.

Sometimes we don't need more light.

We need fewer distractions.

We need a space where we can shut out the noise,

close our eyes,

and talk to God without feeling observed.

Whether it's before a big decision, a hard conversation, an interview, or a scary season, sometimes you need to make your own quiet, dark place…

So you can hear Him.

Scripture

"Be still, and know that I am God."

— Psalm 46:10

Reflection

- Where in your life do you need to quiet the noise so you can hear God?
- Do you create space to be alone with Him, or are you always distracted?
- What would change if you stopped worrying about who was watching?

Prayer

God, teach me how to be still in Your presence.

Help me create space to hear You, even when life is loud.

Let me shut out what doesn't matter.

So I can listen to what does.

In Jesus' name,

Amen.

SOFT LIFE, STRONG SPIRIT

My idea of a soft life was being a Pilates girly.

Not because I didn't want to work hard,

but because I wanted time.

Flexibility.

Freedom.

I wanted to wake up, go to church, grab a matcha, go to Pilates, and then go to brunch with my friends without feeling rushed, drained, or stressed.

For a while, that's exactly what we did.

Sundays became sacred.

Church. Pilates. Brunch. Fellowship. Laughter.

It felt soft.

It felt peaceful.

It felt aligned.

But what nobody tells you about Pilates is this.

It's brutal.

Those slow, controlled movements?

They burn in places you didn't even know you had.

You're not lifting heavy weights.

You're not jumping or sprinting.

You're just… holding.

Breathing.

Repeating.

And that's what builds strength.

Those petite, graceful Pilates girls?

They're strong because they do the same movements over and over again, correctly.

Not fast.

Not flashy.

Just faithful.

That's when it hit me…

This is exactly how your relationship with God works.

You don't grow spiritually because you prayed hard once.

You grow because you pray daily.

You don't build faith because you read the Bible when life gets hard.

You build faith when you open it, even when things are good.

Spiritual strength comes from repetition.

Not perfection.

Not intensity.

Consistency.

If you only talk to God when you're desperate, you stay weak.

But when you build a habit,

a rhythm,

a routine,

That's when your posture changes.

Your mindset changes.

Your confidence changes.

That's how you become the woman you prayed to be.

A real soft life isn't lazy.

It's disciplined peace.

It's a woman who shows up for God every day,

even when she's tired,

even when she's busy,

even when she doesn't feel like it.

That's how you become unshakable.

That's how you become her.

Scripture

"Let us not become weary in doing good, for at the proper time we will reap a harvest if we do not give up."

— Galatians 6:9

Reflection Questions

- What spiritual habits am I consistent with, and which ones do I avoid?
- Where in my life am I expecting results without repetition?
- Do I spend time with God daily, or only when something is wrong?
- What would change if I treated prayer like a daily workout?
- What kind of "soft life" is God trying to build in me through discipline?

Prayer

God,

Thank You for reminding me that strength doesn't come from doing something once. It comes from showing up again and again. Help me stay faithful in the small things, in the quiet moments, and in the daily discipline of choosing You. Even when I don't feel spiritual, even when I don't feel motivated, even when I'm tired. Build my faith like a muscle, slowly, steadily, and with purpose. I trust that what You're growing in me will be worth the process.

In Jesus' name,

Amen.

HAKUNA MATATA

"Hakuna Matata."

No worries.

That phrase sounds cute when Timon and Pumba sing it.

But there's actually something powerful hiding in it.

When Simba ran away from everything he was supposed to become,

He didn't land in chaos.

He landed in rest.

Eat.

Sleep.

Laugh.

Repeat.

No pressure.

No fear.

No expectations.

And while that wasn't where he was meant to stay forever,

It was where he was meant to heal.

Rest isn't lazy.

Rest is sacred.

You cannot pour from an empty cup.

You cannot think clearly when you're exhausted.

You cannot hear God when your spirit is overwhelmed.

Sometimes, the most spiritual thing you can do

is cancel the plans, turn off the noise,

Crawl into your bed, and breathe.

No makeup.

No explaining.

No proving.

Just peace.

There is nothing wrong with saying:

"Not tonight."

"I'm resting."

"I'm choosing me."

Hakuna Matata.

No worries.

God is still in control.

And when you allow yourself to rest,

You give God space to restore you.

Scripture

"Come to Me, all you who are weary and burdened, and I will give you rest."

—Matthew 11:28

Reflection

- What have I been worrying about that I need to let go of?
- When was the last time I truly rested without guilt?
- What would it look like to give myself permission to pause?

Prayer

God, thank You for being my peace. Help me release the worries that exhaust my mind and spirit. Teach me how to rest without guilt, to trust You even when I am still. Restore me, renew me, and let me wake up strengthened.

Amen.

EXPECTATIONS

Going to college after high school is the right thing to do if that's the path meant for you.

That's something I had to learn later in life.

For me, college wasn't presented as a question. It was an expectation. After high school, the only thing anyone asked was, "What college are you going to?" Not if but where. Me and all my friends were on the same track. It was just what you did. It felt like success. It felt like the right thing.

So I went.

And it wasn't like I went for a semester and realized it wasn't for me. I stayed for four years. I had the full HBCU experience, memories, friendships, growth, moments I'll always be grateful for. But somewhere along the way, I realized something hard: this wasn't what I wanted. I was doing it for my parents. For the image of success. For the idea that they had "made it" if their child went to college.

What I really wanted was entrepreneurship, creativity, and building something of my own, which didn't require a traditional education at that moment. But by the time I understood that, I was already deep in it. Deep in expectation. Deep in commitment. And deep in student loan debt, I had to carry on my own.

Sometimes I wish someone had paused with me. Asked me what I wanted. Encouraged me to take a year to explore, to breathe, to listen to myself before jumping into a lifelong financial decision. Maybe I would've still gone. Maybe I wouldn't have. But at least the choice would've been mine.

That lesson stays with me now as a parent. I don't want to force a path on my son just because it looks right on paper. If his journey doesn't require a traditional college education, I want him to know that doesn't make him behind or wrong. Purpose isn't one-size-fits-all.

Grace teaches us that it's okay to outgrow paths we chose before we fully knew ourselves. And wisdom teaches us to pass that freedom forward.

Scripture

"Trust in the Lord with all your heart and lean not on your own understanding; in all your ways submit to Him, and He will make your paths straight."

— Proverbs 3:5–6

Reflection Questions

- Where have you followed expectation instead of alignment?
- What choices in your life were made for approval rather than purpose?
- How can you extend yourself grace for what you didn't know then?

Prayer

God, thank You for the lessons that come with time and reflection. Help me trust You with my path and give me wisdom to choose alignment over expectation, both for myself and for those I lead.

Amen.

SUCCESSFUL, BUT STILL SEARCHING

After leaving college, I stopped saying what I needed and started watching what everyone else was doing, trying to discover what I could do that made sense on the outside. Entrepreneurship felt like the answer. Fitness came naturally to me. I enjoyed it. So I leaned into it.

I went to a personal training school. Got certified in personal training and nutrition. I started Fantasy Fitness, training friends, running sessions, and building momentum. For a moment, it felt good. Like I was finally doing something for myself. Like I was on my way.

But not long after, something felt off.

I added more. A cleaning company. Commercial buildings. A rental property with tenants. Boot camps for women. I was busy. Productive. Making money. From the outside, it looked like success. I was an entrepreneur. A business owner. Doing what people said you were supposed to do.

And yet I wasn't fulfilled.

I knew I was capable. I knew I could grow what I was building. Other people would've been content there. But deep down, I felt like I was still trying to prove something. Still trying to look established. Still chasing something that made me feel legitimate instead of something that made me feel aligned.

What I didn't understand then was that you can be gifted at something and still not be called to it. You can be good at building things and still be building the wrong thing. Fulfillment doesn't come from being impressive; it comes from being obedient to who God created you to be.

That season taught me that success without purpose still leaves you empty. And that searching isn't a failure, it's part of the calling process.

Scripture

"What good is it for someone to gain the whole world, yet forfeit their soul?"

— Mark 8:36

Reflection Questions

- Where have you been successful but still felt unfulfilled?
- What are you doing because it looks right versus what feels aligned?
- How might God be using this season to redirect, not reject you?

Prayer

God, help me stop chasing what looks good and start listening for what is true. Give me patience in seasons of searching and clarity to recognize my calling when You reveal it.

Amen.

THE SMALLEST IN THE ROOM

A friend invited me to an event she was hosting at her event rental space. The space was beautiful, just like the women in the room. It was a gathering for fellowship, networking, and open conversation about life and purpose. As the room filled, I realized I was surrounded by some of the most incredible Black women opening schools, closing on properties, running real estate firms, building legacies in real time.

And I felt small.

Not because of how I looked. Not because I didn't belong. But because of where I felt I was in my life. I thought I was doing okay until I started listening. Listening to what everyone else was working on, dreaming about, building. And when it was my turn to speak, something in me panicked.

I didn't know what I wanted to do next. I was still discovering myself. And instead of standing confidently in where I was, I inflated where I was going. I spoke about opening a gym in Pittsburgh, not because it was a clear vision or something I was actively pursuing, but because I felt like I needed to say something. I needed to sound like I belonged in the room.

What hurts the most about that moment is this: I already had so much I could've spoken about. I had been a landlord. I owned a home. I had boot camps running. I had a good job. I owned a commercial cleaning franchise that was doing extremely well at the time. None of that felt like enough in that moment because comparison had quietly shifted my perspective.

It wasn't a manifestation. It was insecurity.

That experience taught me how easy it is to minimize your real accomplishments when you're surrounded by people doing different things. Grace showed me later that I didn't need to add to my story to make it valuable. I just needed to own it.

Belonging doesn't require exaggeration. Purpose doesn't need a performance. And your season doesn't lose value just because someone else's looks different.

Scripture

"Let each one test his own work, and then his reason to boast will be in himself alone and not in his neighbor."

— Galatians 6:4

Reflection Questions

- When have you felt pressure to present more than where you truly were?
- How does comparison affect the way you see your own accomplishments?
- What would it look like to stand confidently in your current season?

Prayer

God, help me resist the urge to perform for belonging. Teach me to value where I am without comparing it to where others are. Give me the courage to speak the truth and walk confidently on my own path. Amen.

SOMEONE ELSE'S DREAM

One person's dream is not always your own.

I found myself working two jobs in the tech field at two of the biggest companies in technology and automotive technology. Jobs people pray for. Jobs people would gladly trade places to have. One I'd been at for nine years. The other for two. On paper, it looked like favor.

In reality, it was exhausting.

I worked mornings from seven to four. Evenings from five to ten. In between, I was navigating football practices, schedules, meals, and making sure I showed up for my son. I was also trying to show up for God, setting boundaries to protect Sundays, protecting my spirit, protecting what little quiet I had left.

What once felt like answered prayers slowly grew heavy.

I remember how excited I was when I got those job offers. How proud I felt. How sure I was that this was where God wanted me. And maybe it was for that season. But somewhere along the way, the joy faded. Not because the jobs were bad. Not because I wasn't grateful. But because I didn't feel like I was growing.

I started to realize that so much of my time was being spent in places that didn't align with where my heart was going. I was making connections. I was doing good work. But something inside me felt underutilized. Like I was pouring energy into areas that didn't truly align with my purpose.

And that's a hard thing to admit, especially when the world tells you that security equals success.

Grace taught me this: gratitude doesn't require silence. You can be thankful for where God placed you and still recognize when it's time to move differently. A blessing can still become a boundary. An answered prayer can still evolve.

God doesn't waste seasons. Even the ones we outgrow prepare us for what's next.

Scripture

"Whether you turn to the right or to the left, your ears will hear a voice behind you, saying, 'This is the way; walk in it.'"

— Isaiah 30:21

Reflection Questions

- Where have you stayed out of gratitude even though your spirit felt restless?
- How do you discern when a season has served its purpose?
- What boundaries help you protect what matters most right now?

Prayer

God, thank You for the doors You've opened and the lessons You've taught me there. Give me wisdom to know when it's time to stay, when it's time to shift, and how to honor You in every season.

Amen.

WHEN HARD WORK ISN'T ENOUGH

Everywhere I go, I find myself outperforming.

It's not intentional; it's how I was raised. My mom taught me to be grateful for a job. To work hard. To stay. To build a life by showing up every day and giving your best for years, even decades, until retirement. That mindset stayed with me.

But the world changed.

This generation, especially after COVID, moves differently. We're taught to prioritize mental health, growth, and fulfillment. To leave places that don't value us. To stop confusing loyalty with stagnation. And I'm learning that lesson in real time.

At my automotive tech job, I found myself doing the most, far beyond my job description. Creating experiences. Bringing people together. Providing lunches. Building rapport with everyone. Meeting people where they are because that's who I am. I worked from the ground up. I bust my butt. And the work shows on paper and in results.

Yet I watched others do less and move forward faster.

People who made it clear they weren't putting much effort in. People who stayed close to management instead of doing the work. And somehow, they were rewarded. Promoted. Praised. While I was overlooked.

That kind of imbalance messes with you.

It made me doubt myself, not because I didn't know my value, but because I still needed the job. I had bills. A child. Responsibilities. And that tension, needing a job that's draining you while feeling unseen, is a serious mental strain.

It wasn't entitlement. It was fairness. I knew the work I was doing. I could see it. And still, I wasn't being carried the way my effort deserved.

So I leaned on God.

I asked Him to guard my heart from bitterness. To guard my mind from comparison. To remind me that He sees what people overlook. And to move me when the time is right, out of places that no longer align with who I'm becoming.

Grace taught me this: hard work matters, but so does discernment. Just because you can carry a place doesn't mean you're meant to stay there. And just because people don't recognize your effort doesn't mean it's wasted.

God knows what you deserve. And He's faithful to honor work done with integrity, even when others don't.

Scripture

"Whatever you do, work at it with all your heart, as working for the Lord, not for human masters."

— Colossians 3:23

Reflection Questions

- Where have you been giving your best but feeling unseen?
- How do you balance gratitude for provision with honesty about burnout?
- What would it look like to trust God with both your work and your next step?

Prayer

God, thank You for the strength You've given me to work with excellence. Guard my heart when effort goes unnoticed and guide me toward places where my gifts are valued and aligned with Your purpose.

Amen.

WHEN FAITH REQUIRES A LEAP

In this economy, especially in 2026, walking away from a steady income with benefits sounds crazy.

Two jobs. Combined six figures. Stability. Security. On paper, it made no sense to leave. Especially as a single mom. Especially when people are holding onto jobs just to survive.

But I knew something had shifted.

I had reached my peak. I wasn't being valued the way I should've been. I couldn't see a path to growth that aligned with the future I wanted for myself or my family. And deep down, I knew that if I wanted more, if I wanted to create opportunities instead of waiting for them, I would have to step out on faith.

During a short period away to care for my mother, something happened.

This devotional came to me.

I had been trying to find my calling for a long time, and suddenly it became clear: I'm a storyteller. People who know me love it when I enter a room, not because I'm trying to perform, but because I tell stories that make people laugh, cry, and reflect. And I always say, "This isn't comedy, this is my life."

These are real experiences. Real lessons. Real grace.

And I realized maybe this is my purpose. Maybe God didn't take me through everything I've been through just for me to survive it, but to share it. To touch lives quietly, honestly, without needing a big platform or a microphone.

I'm not big on social media. I'm not chasing public speaking stages. But this is my way of saying you can step out on faith and still do well.

I believe in God. And I believe in what He placed inside of me.

Enough to walk away from stability and trust Him to take me to the next level abundantly and intentionally. It may not happen overnight. There may be roadblocks. But that's where faith lives.

Corporate jobs aren't bad. You can grow there. You can go far. But if you feel boxed in… if you feel undervalued… if you know you're capable of building something greater, take the chance.

What's the worst that can happen?

I have a stacked resume. If I need to, I'll work again. I'll do what I have to do. But I refuse to live in fear when I know God didn't call me to play it safe. He called me to trust Him.

God doesn't put His people in positions to lose.

He positions us to win sometimes slowly, sometimes quietly, but always purposefully.

And this season?

This is me taking the step.

Scripture

"Faith by itself, if it is not accompanied by action, is dead."

—James 2:17

Reflection Questions

- Where is fear disguising itself as "wisdom" in your life?
- What gift has God been developing in you through your experiences?
- What would it look like to trust God beyond logic?

Prayer

God, give me the courage to step where You lead, even when it doesn't make sense. Help me trust You beyond numbers, titles, and timelines. I believe You are faithful to finish what You started in me.

Amen.

GOD MET ME WHERE I WAS

Going out isn't always bad.

A friend invited me out to Nobu in Atlanta, and at first, I didn't want to go. I wasn't in the right headspace. I had been isolating for a while, staying to myself, trying to navigate life quietly. But something in me knew I needed to get out of the house. So I mustered up the energy, got my hair done, and went anyway.

She told me it was a private event for a new perfume release. When I arrived, I realized I was wearing sneakers. I looked cute, but still.. Sneakers. I hesitated at the door, unsure if I even belonged inside. My friends encouraged me to come in and told me they had met two really nice guys who were talking to them about their church.

That alone sounded strange. Church at Nobu?

But I walked in anyway.

We were introduced to two men who later shared that they were part of a church in Atlanta called The Path. And no, it didn't feel forced. They weren't there to recruit. They were just being who they were. They invited the three of us to church, and surprisingly, we said yes.

All three of us were battling something. One friend was dealing with postpartum depression. Another was grieving the loss of her brother. And me, I was navigating isolation, transition, and learning how to live in a city where I still felt alone.

So we went.

When we pulled up to the church, guess who was working the front door? The same two men from Nobu. They greeted us like family. The church was small. Intimate. Young. A lot of college students. It felt raw. Honest. More like learning than performance. More like conversation than spectacle.

Something about that stuck with me.

God didn't meet me in isolation. He didn't wait for me to have it all together. He met me when I finally said yes to stepping outside, to connection, to curiosity, to showing up as I was.

That night reminded me that God isn't confined to places we label as "holy." He meets us where we are, in restaurants, in conversations, and in invitations we almost turn down. And sometimes, the step that feels the smallest, just going out, is the one that opens the door to something much bigger.

Scripture

"The Lord directs the steps of the godly. He delights in every detail of their lives."

— Psalm 37:23

Reflection Questions

- Where have you almost said no to something that could've changed your direction?
- How has God met you in unexpected places or moments?
- What might happen if you stayed open to connection instead of retreating?

Prayer

God, thank You for meeting me where I am, not where I think I should be. Help me stay open to Your movement in unexpected places and trust that You are guiding my steps, even when I don't see it clearly yet.

Amen.

CHOOSING CONVICTION OVER COMFORT

After being at the church for some time, I could feel the change in me. I was gravitating toward God in a way I never had before. I made a decision, I wanted to get baptized.

I didn't make that decision lightly. About eight weeks before my baptism, I committed to what the church called the Journey Series. Instead of rushing to the water, they paired me with a group of women mentors who walked with me through Bible study, life conversations, and honest discussions about sin, discipline, and what it truly meant to live as a disciple of Christ.

This wasn't just about getting baptized. It was about understanding what I was stepping into.

We talked about how my life would look different. What stewardship meant. What it meant to surrender not just publicly, but daily. And that mattered to me. I had seen too many moments where people declared faith without fully understanding the weight and beauty of the commitment.

This process changed me.

But not everyone agreed with my timing. One of the mentors felt I might be rushing it and that I should wait longer. And I wrestled with that. I listened. I reflected. But deep down, I knew this was my moment. I wasn't acting out of impulse; I was acting out of conviction.

I invited my friends. My baptism became my birthday celebration. It was live-streamed so my family back home could watch. After four years in a new city, trying to find my way, raise my son, and grow alone, this moment felt like alignment.

It meant everything to me that my family got to see me choose God on my own. That my son could witness my growth. That he could see that faith isn't something you have to be born into perfectly, it's something you can step into intentionally, even later in life.

I had always known God. But I didn't know Him like this.

This baptism wasn't about perfection. It was about surrender. About saying yes to a deeper relationship with Christ, even if others questioned my timing. Grace taught me that obedience doesn't always need consensus. Sometimes, it just needs courage.

Scripture

"When he comes, he will prove the world to be in the wrong about sin and righteousness and judgment."

— John 16:8

Reflection Questions

- Where have you felt called to act even when others questioned your timing?
- How has your understanding of faith deepened over time?
- What example are you setting for those watching your walk?

Prayer

God, thank You for meeting me where I was and guiding me into deeper understanding. Give me the courage to follow You with conviction, even when it feels uncomfortable, and help me remain rooted in You as I continue this journey.

Amen.

SECTION 8: THE PIVOT SEASON

OUTGROWN ENVIRONMENTS

Getting baptized really does change you when your heart, mind, and spirit are in the right place.

It wasn't loud. It wasn't instant. But things I once did without a second thought started to sit differently with me. Going back into nightlife to bartend for extra money didn't feel the same. Being surrounded by people indulging in things I no longer fully agreed with didn't feel good anymore, not because I was judging, but because I felt out of place.

Nightclubs. Strip clubs. Drunk conversations. Lust-filled environments. Even casual conversations with friends about men, dating, and choices they were making, things I used to engage in freely, started to weigh on me.

I tried to step back into it anyway. I bartended again. I went out again. And the attention, the lustful pursuit, the energy, the constant gaze rubbed me the wrong way. Not in the way it did before baptism, but in a deeper way. A way that told me: this doesn't align anymore.

And that was confusing.

Because I'm still me.

I still like music. I still love scary movies. I still enjoy concerts. I still laugh. I'm still learning. I didn't get baptized and wake up perfect. I didn't lose my personality or my joy. What changed was my awareness.

I started asking myself, How does this fit with who I'm becoming?

Not Is this allowed?

But Is this feeding me or pulling me backward?

That tension is real. Wanting to honor God without erasing yourself. Wanting to grow without pretending you've arrived. Wanting to live fully while walking faithfully.

This is where grace meets obedience.

My relationship with God is personal. He knows my heart. He knows my struggles. He knows I'm a work in progress. And I remind myself often that discipleship is not about perfection. It's about progression.

I'm learning. I'm unlearning. I'm growing. And every day I choose to move a little closer, that counts.

Grace teaches me this: conviction doesn't condemn, it redirects. And God is patient with the process.

Scripture

"He who began a good work in you will carry it on to completion."

— Philippians 1:6

Reflection Questions

- What environments no longer feel aligned with who you're becoming?
- Where are you experiencing tension between enjoyment and conviction?
- How can you give yourself grace while still honoring your growth?

Prayer

God, thank You for being patient with me as I grow. Help me discern what feeds my spirit and what pulls me away from You. Teach me how to walk with conviction without condemnation, and grace without compromise.

Amen.

FINDING MY WAY

Moving to a new city is scary.

Moving to a new city with a child is even scarier.

I didn't have family there. No built-in support system. No safety net. It was just my son and me. By that time, he was a little older and used to being raised by a single mom who worked. He knew how to let himself into the house if I hadn't gotten home yet. He understood responsibility early. And while that broke my heart at times, it also showed me how resilient he was.

I came to Georgia with a job, the tech job I'd already been at for four years. That gave me stability. And slowly, I started meeting people. Some through work and some through familiar connections from home. One night, I went out with a friend from my hometown to one of Atlanta's biggest nightclubs. The guys we were with said, "You should work here." And just like that, I was introduced to the nightlife scene.

It felt like a good way to meet people. To connect. To build community in a city that felt so big.

This was the 2020 peak of COVID. Everyone was gravitating to Atlanta. The money was fast. The nights were wild. The energy felt like a movie. If you looked up "COVID Atlanta," you'd understand exactly what was happening. At the time, I still had a relationship with God. He's actually what brought me there, but I didn't yet fully understand what I was witnessing. The level of sin. The lust. The way money moved. The darkness mixed with opportunity.

That understanding came later.

What stood out to me even then was this: not everyone was there just to be there. Many of the women I met were mothers like me. Some were waitressing or bartending to pay for school. One friend was working toward becoming a social worker. Everyone had a reason. A plan. A timeline.

And now six years later, I see the fruit of that.

Friends I worked the nightlife are now married. Some are nurses. Some have master's degrees and are doing impactful work in places like D.C. They went in with a purpose, and they got out.

And then there are others who stayed. Still chasing fast money. Still chasing athletes, rappers, the lifestyle, even after the COVID money dried up. I don't judge them. I give them grace. Some people don't know another way. And some seasons are meant to wake you up, not trap you.

That city taught me discernment. It taught me that the environment can expose you to both opportunity and danger. And it reminded me that purpose, not proximity, determines where you end up.

God used that season to show me who I was, what I wanted, and what I didn't. And even in unfamiliar places, He was still guiding my steps.

Scripture

"The Lord will watch over your coming and going both now and forevermore."

— Psalm 121:8

Reflection Questions

- How have unfamiliar environments shaped your growth?
- Where has God protected you even when you didn't fully understand what you were seeing?
- What helps you stay rooted in purpose when temptation or opportunity surrounds you?

Prayer

God, thank You for guiding me through unfamiliar places and teaching me discernment along the way. Help me remain rooted in purpose, extend grace to others, and trust You as I continue to find my way.

Amen.

WHEN PERSPECTIVE WALKS PAST YOU

There was a moment I felt like a complete failure.

I had to shut down my Airbnb, another business idea that just didn't work out. And that day, I was moving furniture into a storage unit by myself. Loading. Unloading. Sweating. Frustrated.

Every box felt heavy, not just physically, but emotionally.

All I could think was:

I really wanted this to work.

That income is gone.

Now I'm paying for storage.

I'm not from here. I don't know anyone.

Nobody's buying this stuff.

It felt like loss stacked on top of loss.

I sat in that frustration while locking up the unit and walking back to my car, That's when perspective met me in the parking lot.

There was a car parked out front. A father sat in the driver's seat. Kids in the back. The windows were kinda covered, so you couldn't see inside. A mother walked out of the storage facility with her son, smiling, carrying toiletries.

It hit me immediately.

They weren't storing extra furniture.

They were storing their life.

All their belongings lived in that unit. They were pulling out toiletries so they could go wash up somewhere, then coming back to put everything away again. Living out of their car. Living out of that storage facility.

And there I was… selfishly calling myself defeated.

I wasn't without shelter.

I wasn't unsafe.

I wasn't without options.

I wasn't failing; I was redirected.

That moment humbled me in a way I'll never forget. It reminded me that sometimes what feels like loss is actually protection. Sometimes God shuts a door not because you weren't capable but because it wasn't meant to carry you forward.

Failure isn't losing something.

Failure is losing perspective.

And God was kind enough to hand me mine that day quietly, without shame, just clarity.

Scripture

"Better is little with the fear of the Lord than great treasure with turmoil."

— Proverbs 15:16

Reflection Questions

- Where have you labeled something as a failure that may actually be a form of redirection?
- Has comparison or frustration blurred your gratitude lately?
- What has God preserved for you, even in disappointment?

Prayer

God, thank You for gently correcting my perspective. Help me see redirection as mercy and closed doors as protection. Teach me gratitude even when things don't go as planned.

Amen.

PERFECTION OBSESSION

This isn't one of my proud moments, but it's an honest one.

I was hosting a party with my friend group, along with another group of women who were a little older than us. The party was for two friends, and the expectation was simple: everyone shows up with something. A dish. A beverage. Help. We all agreed.

I wanted everything to be perfect.

Not just because I was hosting, but because this was a crossover of friend groups. I wanted it to look good. Feel good. Be impressive. And when the other group arrived, they did exactly that. They came early. They came prepared. Platters done perfectly. Drinks ready. Decorations in hand. Matching outfits. Ready to assist without being asked.

Then my friend group started to arrive.

One friend showed up late. No dish. No drink. And on top of that, an attitude. A nonchalant energy that immediately rubbed me the wrong way. I don't know if it was the fact that she didn't bring anything, or the way she carried herself when she arrived, but something in me snapped.

I confronted her.

And what should have been a conversation turned into something bigger. Louder. Messier. A moment I wish I had handled differently. Looking back, I know the reaction wasn't really about the party. It was about everything I was carrying at the time. The pressure. The exhaustion. The need for things to go right when so much else in my life had gone wrong.

Her lack of effort and the casual way she moved through it triggered something deeper in me.

Grace later taught me that unhealed pressure will always find a way to spill. I wasn't angry because the party wasn't perfect. I was angry because I needed it to be. I needed one thing in my life to feel controlled, organized, and respected.

That moment humbled me. It reminded me that perfection is a heavy burden to place on yourself and on others. And that not everyone will show up the way you need them to, even if they care.

Growth looks like recognizing your triggers and taking responsibility for how you respond to them. I couldn't change how she showed up, but I could learn from how I reacted.

Scripture

"So then each of us will give an account of ourselves to God."

— Romans 14:12

Reflection Questions

- When was the last time pressure caused you to react instead of respond?
- What expectations are you placing on others that may really reflect your own stress?
- How can you give yourself grace for moments you wish you'd handled differently?

Prayer

God, help me recognize when I'm operating from pressure instead of peace. Teach me to pause before reacting and to extend grace to others and to myself when things don't go as planned.

Amen.

REJECTION RECHARGE

What is it about rejection that flips a switch in us?

A failed relationship.

A job we really wanted but didn't get.

Being overlooked, dismissed, or underestimated, even in something small.

Why does rejection put a battery in our backs?

Why does it suddenly make us want to level up, grind harder, glow brighter, and prove something?

I've asked myself this a lot.

Is it a point to prove to other people?

Or is it a point to prove to ourselves?

I think it's both, but deeper than that, rejection forces us to see ourselves clearly. It shakes us awake. It confronts us with a question we don't always want to answer:

Do I believe in myself without external validation?

Sometimes rejection hurts because it touches a wound a place where we were already doubting ourselves. Other times, it hurts because we know we're capable, and someone else can't see it.

But here's the part that changed my perspective:

Rejection doesn't create the fire; it reveals it.

The ambition was already there.

The resilience was already there.

The hunger was already there.

Rejection just removes comfort.

And when comfort is gone, clarity shows up.

That "I'll show them" energy isn't always about ego. Sometimes it's about alignment. It's about realizing I don't belong where I'm not valued. It's about God redirecting us, not punishing us.

Not every door that closes is a loss.

Some are protection.

Some are preparation.

Some are simply God saying, "There's more for you; keep going."

And maybe the point isn't to prove anything to anyone else at all.

Maybe the point is to prove to yourself that you won't shrink just because someone couldn't see your worth.

Scripture

"The stone the builders rejected has become the cornerstone."

— Psalm 118:22

Reflection Questions

- When I feel rejected, which emotion comes up first hurt or motivation?
- Who am I really trying to prove something to?
- What if rejection is redirection instead of failure?

Prayer

God, help me not internalize rejection as defeat.

Give me wisdom to recognize when You are closing doors for my protection and opening paths I couldn't yet see.

Help me move forward with confidence, not bitterness.

Amen.

OH, I WANNA MOVE HERE

Why Do We Always Want to Move on Vacation?"

I know I'm not the only one.

Every time I go on vacation, whether it's a quick weekend trip or a big international getaway, I find myself thinking the same thing:

Dang… I want to move here.

Why are we like this?

Why does life always feel lighter away from home?

Maybe it's because when we're on vacation, life is simplified.

No laundry piling up.

No dishes in the sink.

No rushing from one obligation to the next.

Even when we stay somewhere modest, an Airbnb, a small hotel, somewhere unfamiliar, it still feels better. It feels freer. Lighter. More alive.

But the truth is, it's not always the place.

It's the pause.

Vacation gives us permission to rest without guilt.

To enjoy without rushing.

To be present without worrying about what's next.

At home, we're constantly carrying the responsibility of work, bills, schedules, and expectations. On vacation, those things don't disappear, but they quiet down long enough for us to remember what peace feels like.

And sometimes, what we're really longing for isn't a new city or a new country, it's a new pace.

A slower rhythm.

A softer life.

More joy in the everyday.

God doesn't only exist in the escape.

He exists in the ordinary too.

The challenge isn't to move every time we feel inspired, it's to ask ourselves:

What part of this feeling do I need to bring back home with me?

Maybe it's rest.

Maybe it's boundaries.

Maybe it's gratitude.

Maybe it's simply remembering that joy doesn't have to be reserved for plane tickets and passports.

Peace is portable if we let it be.

Scripture

"Better a handful of quietness than two handfuls of toil and chasing after the wind."

— Ecclesiastes 4:6

Reflection Questions

- What specifically makes a vacation feel better for me?
- Is it the place or the lack of pressure?
- What's one thing I can change at home to create more peace in my daily life?

Prayer

God, help me stop chasing peace in places and start cultivating it in my life. Teach me how to rest without running, and how to enjoy the life You've already given me.

Amen.

RICH, BLESSED, AND STILL HUNGRY

There's a rap song called Rich, Blessed & Savage that had my best friend and me in a chokehold one summer. Warning: the song is pretty explicit… Give me grace!

We were throwing her annual pool party, the kind that was always a big deal.

And that night, everything was flowing.

The energy was high.

The money was good.

The vibes were safe.

No drama.

No fights.

Just favor.

We kept playing that song on repeat, and it felt like it became a prophecy.

We were rich not just in money, but in opportunity.

We were blessed, protected, covered, and surrounded by good energy.

And we were savage, not reckless, but hungry.

And that word stuck with me.

Because being savage doesn't mean being mean.

It means being determined.

Focused.

Unwilling to stay small.

I want to be rich, but not just financially.

I want to be rich in peace.

In love.

In freedom.

In joy.

I want to be blessed not just with things, but with protection, discernment, and alignment.

And I want to stay savage, hungry for more.

More growth.

More healing.

More God.

More purpose.

Savage means I protect my spirit.

I guard my ear.

I don't let distractions steal my destiny.

Savage means I don't settle.

So yes, I want wealth.

But I also want God's hand on it.

I want overflow without losing my soul.

Rich.

Blessed.

And still hungry.

Scripture

"May he give you the desires of your heart and make all your plans succeed"

— Psalm 20:4

Reflection

- What does "rich" mean to me beyond money?
- Where in my life do I need to stay hungry rather than get comfortable?
- How can I protect my blessings while still pursuing more?

Prayer

God, make me rich in the ways that matter.

Bless me without adding sorrow.

Keep me hungry for what You have for me.

Let me never grow lazy in my purpose.

Amen.

NEW CAR FAITH

You don't really understand faith until you're sitting in a car dealership…

Waiting to see if your credit will hold up.

This was one of those moments.

My car had just been totaled in a hit-and-run, so I did what I could. I called my bank and got preapproved for a loan. I felt ready. Covered. Confident.

Now here's the funny part.

It was my best friend's birthday, my best friend since kindergarten, and she needed a car too. Unlike me, she hadn't done the preapproval. No paperwork. No plan. Just faith.

So I asked her what she wanted to do for her birthday.

She said, "We're getting matching cars."

Without hesitation, I said, "Cool. Matching Jeeps."

We walked into dealership after dealership.

Cars overpriced. Numbers not making sense.

Every stop felt like a "no."

But we didn't panic.

We didn't complain.

We just kept the faith.

Finally, at the third dealership, we found the same model, one year apart, brand new, zero miles. The salesman was locked in. We were locked in.

Nine hours.

Nine hours of waiting, praying, trusting, and refusing to walk out discouraged.

We didn't care about money down.

We didn't obsess over credit scores.

We didn't let logic override belief.

We trusted God.

And somehow, favor found us.

We walked out of the dealership with matching Jeep Wranglers on her birthday, exactly as she imagined.

Was that how she planned to spend her birthday? Probably not.

But was it unforgettable? Absolutely.

Faith doesn't always look dramatic.

Sometimes it looks like patience.

Sometimes it looks like stubborn hope.

Sometimes it looks like sitting in a plastic chair under fluorescent lights, trusting God anyway.

And when God shows up, He shows out.

Scripture

"Now faith is the substance of things hoped for, the evidence of things not seen."

— Hebrews 11:1

Reflection Questions

- When was the last time I trusted God without knowing the outcome?
- Do I let fear stop me before faith has a chance?
- What would it look like to believe fully, even in practical situations?

Prayer

God, help me trust You not just in the big moments, but in the everyday decisions.

Teach me to walk by faith, even when the numbers don't make sense.

Thank You for the favor I didn't earn and the blessings I didn't see coming.

Amen.

YOU THINK YOU ALL THAT

"You think you all that."

That statement always makes me smile because yes…

I do.

Not in an arrogant way.

Not in a look-down-on-others way.

But in a God-confidence way.

I know whose daughter I am.

I know who covers me.

I know who orders my steps.

When people say that to you, it's rarely about you.

It's about how your confidence makes them uncomfortable.

It exposes what they don't yet see in themselves.

You don't have to announce your worth.

You don't have to convince anyone.

The way you walk.

The way you move.

The way you protect your peace.

The way you believe in yourself it already speaks.

And when someone feels small next to someone who knows who they are,

They call it "cocky."

But heaven calls it faith.

Scripture

"So do not throw away your confidence; it will be richly rewarded."

— Hebrews 10:35

Reflection

- Do you ever shrink to make others comfortable?
- Where in your life do you need to stand taller instead of quieter?
- What would change if you fully believed you were worthy?

Prayer

God, thank You for reminding me who I am.

Let me walk in confidence that comes from You, not from comparison.

Help me never shrink myself to fit someone else's comfort zone.

Teach me to stand tall in who You created me to be.

In Jesus' name,

Amen.

WORLD READY VS. WORD READY

People always say things like,

"You give wife."

"You've got wifey energy."

And for a long time, I tried to figure out what that really meant.

Yes, I can cook.

I keep a clean home.

I carry myself with dignity.

I take care of my child.

I'm educated.

I'm respectful.

I don't move recklessly.

I'm not in everybody's DMs.

I don't entertain chaos.

By the world's standards, I look ready.

But I'm still single.

And it finally hit me…

It's not because I wasn't doing the right things outwardly.

It's because I wasn't prepared inwardly.

I wasn't rooted in the Word enough to be aligned with what God calls a wife to be.

I knew how to look like a wife,

But I didn't yet understand the sacrifices, discipline, humility, submission, leadership, and spiritual covering that real marriage requires.

In the world, I was ready.

But in the Word, I wasn't.

And that's why God protected me from stepping into something I wasn't spiritually prepared to carry.

This isn't just about marriage.

It's about everything.

You can look ready for success…

but not be spiritually equipped to sustain it.

You can look like a leader…

but not be rooted enough to lead.

You can look healed…

but still be carrying wounds.

God doesn't just prepare us for what we want.

He prepares us for what we can keep.

Scripture

"Unless the Lord builds the house, the builders labor in vain."

— Psalm 127:1

Reflection Questions

- Am I preparing for what I want according to the world or according to God?
- What areas of my life look ready on the outside but still need spiritual work on the inside?
- If God gave me what I asked for today, would I be equipped to sustain it?

Prayer

God, thank You for protecting me from stepping into things I wasn't spiritually ready to carry.

Help me not rush what looks good in the world while neglecting what You are building in me in secret.

Prepare my heart, my spirit, and my discipline for the future You are designing for me.

Align me with Your Word so that when the blessing comes, I can keep it.

In Jesus' name, Amen.

SECTION 9: FINISH STRONG

CLEAN THAT CAR

I always tell myself this:

God is not going to bless me with more if I don't take care of what I already have.

You have to be a good steward of your life, your finances, your home, your car, your relationships, your time. Everything you have right now is already a blessing. And how you treat what you have is a reflection of how you'll treat what's coming.

I think about this every time the Powerball reaches a billion dollars. Everybody starts dreaming, myself included.

"If I won, I'd do this."

"I'd give this."

"I'd change everything."

We start negotiating with God as if He doesn't already know our habits.

But the truth is, if I had perfect money management, I wouldn't be in the position I'm in right now. If I were disciplined, if I were consistent, if I truly knew how to steward abundance, I'd already be living differently.

We all want more.

A bigger house.

A newer car.

More money.

More opportunity.

But look around.

Is the car you already have clean?

Are the tires rotated?

Is the oil changed?

Is the check-engine light on?

Is your house in order?

Are the clothes folded?

Is the space peaceful?

Is it cared for?

Is your money respected?

Or is TikTok Shop, Klarna, Afterpay, and impulse spending draining you every week?

Why would God give you more if you don't honor what you already have?

Stewardship comes before overflow.

When you take care of what's in your hands now, you show God you're ready for what's next.

So clean that car.

Organize that house.

Fix your habits.

Respect your money.

Your blessing is already on the way; it's just waiting for you to make room for it.

Scripture

"Whoever can be trusted with very little can also be trusted with much, and whoever is dishonest with very little will also be dishonest with much."

—Luke 16:10

Reflection

- What is one thing in my life that I haven't been taking care of the way I should?
- How can I better steward what I already have?
- What habits might be blocking me from receiving more?

Prayer

God, thank You for everything You have already given me.

Forgive me for the times I've taken Your blessings for granted.

Teach me how to be a good steward of my finances, my home, my time, and my resources.

Help me to honor what I have now so I can be trusted with more.

I'm making room for the blessings You're preparing for me.

In Jesus' name, Amen.

BIRTHDAYS BEHIND BARS

I'll casually say it in conversation, "I went to jail once," and people never believe me.

I don't go into detail. I usually just dismiss it. Sometimes I don't even believe it myself.

But it happened.

A simple traffic violation from college, something minor, something I never thought twice about, turned into a warrant I didn't even know existed. Years later, just days before my 21st birthday, I went downtown to pick up my gun license. Back then, you had to go under the courthouse to the sheriff's office, show your yellow card, and pick it up in person.

Instead, they told me I had a warrant out for my arrest.

They called the judge from Delaware County.

The judge said he wanted to see me in person.

That one moment landed me in jail for over a month.

I spent my 21st birthday behind bars.

Christmas behind bars.

New Year's behind bars.

While my friends were at the club celebrating me with tiered cakes, full-body cutouts, and a whole party thrown in my honor, I was sitting in a cell in the Allegheny County Jail.

Eventually, I was extradited to Delaware County, had my court hearing, and was immediately released.

Just like that.

And I remember thinking: Why?

Why this?

Why now?

While I was in jail, I met women from every walk of life.

Young girls locked up for prostitution.

Teachers doing 90 days for their third DUI.

Mothers missing their kids during the holidays.

Women who made one bad decision or a series of them and were now paying for it.

And somehow, even in that place, God had me doing what I always do.

Talking. Encouraging. Pouring into people.

Telling young girls:

You're beautiful.

This isn't for you.

You don't have to accept this life.

You don't have to deal with men who don't value you.

Looking back, I know exactly why God put me there.

He slowed me down.

I was living fast. Careless. Comfortable. One step away from something far worse. Jail wasn't punishment; it was protection.

And He used me.

Even in a place I never thought I'd be, God still gave me purpose. Even locked behind a door, I wasn't useless. I wasn't forgotten.

I was placed.

Sometimes God will interrupt your life so loudly that you can't ignore Him anymore. Not to shame you but to save you.

Scripture

"Before I was afflicted I went astray, but now I obey your word."

— Psalm 119:67

Reflection Questions

- Has God ever stopped you abruptly to protect you from something worse?
- Can you see moments in your past that felt like punishment but were actually mercy?
- How might God have used you in places you never expected to be?

Prayer

God, thank You for protecting me even when I didn't understand it. Thank You for slowing me down, for placing me where You needed me, and for never wasting a moment of my life. Help me trust You even when the interruption hurts. Amen.

SARAH

My first cellmate in jail was an OG named Sarah.

We had spent three days downstairs in the holding cell before finally being processed upstairs. By that point, I knew I wasn't getting out anytime soon. No lawyer. No money. No phone calls from family. Nothing could move it.

I had to sit.

Sarah was a middle-aged white woman. You could tell she had once lived a normal life, a home, kids, routines, but addiction had clearly taken its toll. We didn't talk much at first. I judged her quietly. I was young, confused, and terrified.

Then it was time to go upstairs.

We were walked past pod after pod glass walls where inmates could see us. And everywhere we passed, people were shouting:

"Sarah!"

"What's up, girl?"

"Love you, Sarah!"

Everyone knew her.

When we got to our cell, guess who my roommate was?

Sarah.

She let me choose the bunk. She showed me how to set up my tiny space. She spoke gently. She told me everything would be okay.

She had come prepared; she knew she was coming to jail. She wore layers of white clothing so she could keep them rather than wear one pair of jail scrubs. She knew the system.

Then she did something I'll never forget.

It was my 21st birthday.

My real birthday party was happening on the outside, and somehow, I still don't know how Sarah managed to get a small radio. My name was being shouted out on the air while I was locked in a cell.

I cried.

The next day she said, "We're throwing you a birthday party in here."

And with nothing but what she had, she brought me a Snickers and a Twix.

"This is for you," she said. "I know it's not much."

But it was everything.

In a place built to strip people of dignity, Sarah gave me humanity.

And I learned something that day:

You never know who God will use to show you grace.

Sometimes it's not the people who look safe.

Sometimes it's not the ones who look put together.

Sometimes it's the broken ones who understand how to love the deepest.

Scripture

"Do not judge, or you too will be judged. For in the same way you judge others, you will be judged, and with the measure you use, it will be measured to you."

— Matthew 7:1-2

Reflection Questions

- Who have I judged before truly knowing their heart?
- When has God sent me help through someone unexpected?
- How can I offer grace the way Sarah did, even with a little?

Prayer

God, thank You for the people You send when I feel alone.

Help me see others the way You see them, not by their past, but by their heart.

Teach me to give grace, even when it's inconvenient.

Amen.

SEEING THE PERSON NOT THE PRISON

One of the people I stayed in contact with from that season in jail was a young woman named Stevie.

We eventually found each other on Facebook years later, but the way we met was nothing short of surreal.

When I was extradited from Pittsburgh to Delaware County, they treated me like I was some big-time criminal. Shackles on my ankles. Handcuffs on my wrists. Two officers dedicated just to me, driving six to seven hours across the state. When I arrived, they didn't process me as someone coming from another jail. They processed me as if I had just walked in off the street.

I was placed back into a holding cell, still in my outside clothes, with people who were just arriving.

That's where I met Stevie.

Across from us, you could see the men's holding area. Her boyfriend or fiancé was over there. They were both clearly strung out, angry, and aggressive with the C.O.'s. I don't even remember what landed them there. What I remember is how fiercely she was trying to protect him.

Once we were moved upstairs into the pods, people kept their distance from her. Nobody really befriended her. You could tell she had lived hard; her face showed it. She looked like she had lived ten lifetimes, even though she was my age, maybe younger.

But I didn't see what everyone else saw.

I saw a person.

So I leaned in.

I talked to her. I listened. I wanted to know her story. Not her charges. Not her addiction. Her.

And we formed a small connection in a place where connections are rare.

Eventually, I was released. Stevie stayed. I think she did more time, maybe even years. Life moved on.

Then one day, we found each other on Facebook.

And I barely recognized her.

She looked healthy. Clean. She had children. She was a loving mother. I don't even know if she was still with the same man, but I do know she was alive, thriving, and standing in a completely different place than where I met her.

And that moment stuck with me deeply.

Because I had seen her before she could see herself.

Not as a drug addict.

Not as an angry woman.

Not as a problem.

But as someone with value.

Sometimes people don't need fixing. They need to be seen.

And I believe God lets us cross paths with people in their darkest moments, not so we can judge them, but so we can reflect back to them a version of themselves they can't yet imagine.

Scripture

"Be merciful, just as your Father is merciful."

— Luke 6:36

Reflection Questions

- Have you ever been seen by someone when you were at your lowest?
- Are there people in your life God may be calling you to see differently?
- Who might need to borrow your faith until they find their own?

Prayer

God, help me see people the way You see them. Strip away my judgment, my fear, and my assumptions. Let me be a mirror of hope for someone who can't yet see their own worth.

Amen.

Cancer WHO?

Finding out your mom has breast cancer is heavy, especially when your mom is the matriarch.

She's the glue.

The cook for every holiday.

The one everyone runs to when life falls apart.

The safe place.

The provider when money is tight.

The one who never stops showing up.

So when she told me she had breast cancer, it shook the room even if I didn't let it show.

She told me first. Not because I was her favorite, but because she believed I was the most mentally stable. She needed me to carry it. She needed me to tell my siblings. And I could see it on her face that she had been sitting with this for days, unsure how to tell her children, almost as if she thought it was a death sentence.

But I didn't receive it that way.

My first reaction wasn't panic. It wasn't fear. It wasn't stress. And I think that surprised her. I could tell she was waiting for me to break, but I didn't. Because worry is not trusting God.

So I made it light.

I said, "Well girl, I guess we're about to beat breast cancer."

I joked about pink for October.

I reminded her how many women survive it.

How there's a whole month dedicated to survivors.

I told her this was just another chapter, another testimony.

Was I scared? Of course.

Did I feel it? Absolutely.

But I refused to let fear lead.

I kept it light because I knew she needed strength more than sympathy. I kept it light as I walked into surgery. I kept it light walking out. I even kept it light when telling my siblings because I already knew how they would react, and I knew someone had to anchor the room.

Faith doesn't mean pretending things don't hurt.

Faith means deciding who gets the final word.

This diagnosis didn't break us; it brought us closer. It became another journey we walked through together as a family. And now, we're one of the fortunate ones. We get to say my mom survived breast cancer.

Not everyone gets that testimony.

Grace taught me this: sometimes faith looks like laughter in a hospital room. Sometimes it looks like choosing hope before fear can speak. And sometimes it looks like being strong, not because you aren't scared, but because you trust God more than you trust the diagnosis.

Scripture

"God is our refuge and strength, an ever-present help in trouble."

— Psalm 46:1

Reflection Questions

- How do you respond when fear tries to take control?
- Who has God called you to be strong for, even when you're hurting too?
- What testimony might God be writing through a season that feels scary?

Prayer

God, thank You for being present in moments that feel overwhelming. Help me lead with faith, speak life when fear tries to rise, and trust You fully, no matter the diagnosis or the circumstance.

Amen.

LOGGING OUT TO TUNE IN

Social media is one of the wildest places we live in.

You can open your phone and see a powerful Bible verse…

And two scrolls later, you're looking at something that doesn't align with your spirit at all.

A miracle. A tragedy. A thirst trap. A war. A wedding. A breakup.

All within thirty seconds.

That's a lot for the human mind and soul to process.

Social media isn't evil.

It's actually powerful; you can build businesses, meet people, share your story, and inspire others.

But it's also one of the biggest tools of distraction and comparison.

Scrolling turns into zoning out.

Zoning out turns into self-doubt.

Self-doubt turns into losing focus.

Sometimes you don't realize how much noise is in your head until you finally unplug.

There are seasons when God needs you to be quiet.

Not because you're falling behind

But because you're about to move forward.

When you step back from social media, you give your spirit room to breathe.

You hear God more clearly.

You think more clearly.

You move more intentionally.

And when you come back?

You come back as a more focused, grounded, aligned version of yourself.

Scripture

""And whatever you do, whether in word or deed, do it all in the name of the Lord Jesus..."

— Colossians 3:17

Reflection Questions

- How much time am I spending consuming other people's lives instead of building my own?
- Does social media leave me feeling inspired… or insecure?
- What would it look like to take a break and realign my focus with God?
- What could I create if I replaced scrolling with stillness?

Prayer

God, help me guard my eyes, my mind, and my spirit.

Show me when I need to disconnect so I can reconnect with You.

Remove anything that distracts me from the purpose you've placed in my life.

Teach me to use platforms wisely, not let them use me.

Quiet the noise so I can hear You clearly.

Refocus my heart so I can move forward boldly.

In Jesus' name, Amen.

I CAN'T FAIL

Using music to shift your mindset is one of the simplest ways to give yourself grace. Sometimes a song can pull you out of a heavy moment, remind you of your blessings, or give you the motivation you need to keep going.

Now I'll be honest I'm still a new Christian. I'm still learning. I'm still unlearning. I'm still figuring out the balance between what feeds my spirit and what just feeds my vibe. So no, I'm not going to pretend that I never listen to secular music. But I do believe that even in unexpected places, God can drop wisdom if your heart is open.

One of my favorite songs by Jay-Z and Beyoncé is Nice. And one line has stayed with me for years:

"What would you do if you knew you couldn't fail?"

That question will change the way you look at everything.

Because fear only exists when we think failure is an option.

When you remove failure from the equation, suddenly your dreams don't seem so crazy.

Suddenly, your prayers don't feel so unrealistic.

Suddenly stepping out on faith feels… possible.

What would you do if you really believed God had your back?

You would apply for that job.

You would start that business.

You would walk away from what no longer serves you.

You would love deeper.

You would dream bigger.

When you know you are held by a powerful God, confidence isn't arrogance; it's trust.

Not in yourself alone… but in the God who placed the vision inside you.

Scripture

"Have I not commanded you? Be strong and courageous. Do not be afraid; do not be discouraged, for the Lord your God will be with you wherever you go."

—Joshua 1:9

Reflection

- What have you been afraid to try because you're scared of failing?
- If failure wasn't possible, what would you go after today?
- What is God calling you to step into with boldness?

Prayer

God, thank You for reminding me that fear doesn't get the final say. You do.

Help me to see myself the way You see me: capable, chosen, and covered.

Give me the courage to move forward even when I don't have all the answers.

Teach me to trust that if You placed the dream in my heart, You will also give me the strength to walk it out.

In Jesus' name, Amen.

SIDE QUEST

Me and my girls were talking about how we want this year to look different not just in the big goals, but in the little joys too. Someone mentioned doing "side quests," and it stuck with me.

If you've ever played video games, you know what a side quest is. It's not the main mission; it's the optional adventure. The extra path you take that yields skills, connections, and unexpected rewards.

One of my friends said her side quests this year were learning to play tennis, equestrian, and play golf.

I said… equestrian? Like, horses?

Where do you even find that?

But she was serious. She researched it. She signed up. She committed.

And that made me realize something: side quests are how you build a fuller life.

They're not about proving anything.

They're about expanding yourself.

Your side quest might be:

Gardening so you get more sun and peace

Pickleball where you meet new people

Salsa dancing because you want to feel alive again

A book club

A cooking class

A language app

A gym you've never tried

You never know what God has waiting for you in rooms you've never entered.

Your next business partner could be in a tennis class.

Your next job referral could be at Pilates.

Your future husband could be learning how to dance beside you.

God doesn't bless comfort zones. He blesses movement.

Side quests pull you out of isolation.

They bring you into new conversations, new environments, and new energy.

They remind you that life is meant to be explored, not just survived.

And when I look back now, I realize something…

This book was never my main plan.

It started as a side quest.

A little writing.

A little reflecting.

A little obedience.

And now… here I am.

Sometimes the thing you start "just for fun" becomes the thing that changes your life.

Scripture

"The Lord had said to Abram, 'Go from your country, your people and your father's household to the land I will show you."

— Genesis 12:1

Reflection

- What is one thing you've been curious about but keep putting off?
- Where could God be trying to expand you through joy instead of pressure?
- Who might you meet if you stepped outside your normal routine?
- What part of you is waiting to be awakened through something new?
- Are you willing to let a "side quest" become part of your calling?

Prayer

God, thank You for reminding me that my life is more than survival; it is meant to be explored. Help me say yes to new experiences, new spaces, and new versions of myself. Open doors through curiosity, joy, and courage. Lead me into rooms that grow me, stretch me, and connect me to the people and opportunities You've prepared for me. I trust that even my side quests are part of Your divine plan.

Amen.

THE FIRST TIME I BET ON MYSELF

I always say my first real business was when I was ten years old.

Before that, I had little hustles selling icy cups, shoveling snow, doing anything a kid could do to make a few dollars. But when my mom asked me what I wanted for Christmas that year, I didn't say a toy. I didn't say a bike. I said, "I want a candy store."

And she made it happen.

She found shelving units. We set them up in the landing area of our house. She took me to Sam's Club and to the old candy store on the South Side to buy penny candies, Frooties, lemon cookies, Chico Sticks, Boston Baked Beans, all the nostalgic stuff. Before we knew it, I was open for business.

And the crazy part? I had recognized a real need.

There was no candy store in my neighborhood. Just a house that sold alcohol, the ice cream truck, and a long walk to the nearest corner store. So I filled the gap.

That was entrepreneurship before I even knew the word.

Fast-forward into adulthood, and that same spirit never left me.

I opened a commercial cleaning franchise that still runs today.

I tried personal training.

Activewear.

Real estate.

Airbnbs.

Mobile bartending.

Property management.

And now… this.

Some things worked.

Some didn't.

Some taught me what I didn't want.

Some showed me what I was capable of.

But the common denominator in all of it?

I kept trying.

Entrepreneurship isn't about never failing. It's about never stopping.

Trying. Pivoting. Learning. Adjusting. Starting again.

God doesn't give you ideas for nothing.

He plants them in you because there is provision attached to them, even if it doesn't show up in the way or the season you expected.

You don't always get it right the first time. But you don't get anywhere at all if you never start.

Scripture

"Commit to the Lord whatever you do, and he will establish your plans."

— Proverbs 16:3

Reflection Questions

- What is something God placed on my heart that I've been afraid to try?
- Am I quitting too early when things get hard?
- What patterns do I see in the things I'm drawn to create?
- What would happen if I trusted God enough to take the next step?

Prayer

God, thank You for being a God of new beginnings and second chances.

Thank You for the ideas You place in my spirit, even when I don't fully understand them yet.

Help me not be afraid to try, even if it means failing.

Teach me how to pivot without giving up.

Remind me that You are guiding my steps, even when the path looks unclear.

I trust that what You planted in me has purpose.

Give me the courage to keep going. In Jesus' name, Amen.

THIS IS THE DAY

"This is the day that the Lord has made.

We will rejoice and be glad in it."

We've reached the end, and yet somehow, this feels like the beginning.

Through these pages, you've seen yourself.

You've remembered who you were.

You've confronted who you are.

And you've leaned into who God is shaping you to become.

You came.

You saw.

You conquered.

You lost.

You loved.

You healed.

You broke.

You grew.

And through all of it, God never left.

The fact that you picked up this book wasn't random.

The fact that you stayed with it wasn't an accident.

And the fact that you finished it means something shifted inside you.

God met you here.

This journey wasn't about perfection.

It wasn't about having all the answers.

It was about alignment.

About waking up and choosing God again and again.

About learning how to listen.

About learning how to trust.

About learning how to stand in grace even when life didn't make sense.

We are not alone.

Every woman reading this carries her own story, her own wounds, her own faith.

Different paths.

Same God.

And at the center of it all is the playbook we were given.

the Word,

the truth,

the cheat code,

the shortcut,

the compass.

God.

He is the source of peace.

The source of joy.

The source of clarity.

The source of abundance.

And when you align with Him, everything else finds its place.

So wherever you are right now

whether you're just beginning,

just healing,

just dreaming,

or just surviving

know this:

You are not behind.

You are not forgotten.

You are not lost.

You are exactly where God can use you.

And this…

This is the day the Lord has made.

Rejoice in it.

Walk boldly into what's next.

And never forget

Your story is still being written.

Scripture

"This is the day the Lord has made; let us rejoice and be glad in it."

—Psalm 118:24

Closing Prayer

God, thank You for meeting me in this journey.

Thank You for the growth, the tears, the healing, and the faith.

As I move forward, let me stay aligned with You.

Guide my steps, guard my heart, and bless every season ahead.

Amen.

FINAL REFLECTION

Before you close this book, take one last moment with God.

Write honestly. Write gently. Write without performance.

1. What did God reveal to me in these 90 days?

2. What am I releasing in this next season?

3. What am I becoming and what does it require of me?

4. What habit, truth, or Scripture am I taking with me?

5. Where do I need to give myself grace more often?

6. What is one prayer I'm carrying forward from this journey?

ABOUT THE AUTHOR

Tandra Wade is a writer, entrepreneur, and devoted mother whose work centers on faith, growth, and becoming. Through her writing, she invites readers into an honest and grace- filled journey of spiritual formation rooted in real life, real questions, and real transformation.

As a woman navigating new faith, leadership, purpose, and personal development, Tandra writes from lived experience rather than perfection. Her work reflects a deep belief that faith is not built overnight, but formed gradually through obedience, reflection, and trust in God's process. *Faith in the Making* was created to support women in seasons of transition those learning to walk with God while building families, businesses, and futures at the same time.

Tandra's writing is marked by clarity, warmth, and relatability, offering encouragement without pressure and conviction without condemnation. Her goal is to create space for readers to grow spiritually while extending themselves grace understanding that becoming is as sacred as arrival.

In addition to writing, Tandra is actively involved in entrepreneurship and community building. She is passionate about helping women pursue purpose with faith at the center and believes that a surrendered life leads to lasting transformation.

Faith in the Making is her invitation to walk alongside readers as they grow one day, one prayer, and one step of faith at a time.

Published by **Apex Pillars Group LLC**

STAY CONNECTED

If this devotional encouraged you, I'd love to hear from you.

Leave a review and share this book with a woman who's still trying.
Your support helps this message reach the right heart at the right time.

Connect with me here:
Email: info@apexpillars.com

Tik Tok: @FaithInTheMakingTV

Youtube: @FaithInTheMakingTV

Instagram: @FaithInTheMakingTV

AUTHOR'S BLESSING

May you leave these pages lighter than you came.

*May you stop replaying the parts of your story God already redeemed,
and start expecting the parts He's still writing.*

*May grace find you in the morning
before your thoughts get loud,
before the world starts pulling on you,
before you start believing you have to earn what God already promised.*

*May your healing be steady.
May your growth be honest.
May your faith be rooted
not in how you feel,
but in who God is.*

*May you become the kind of person who doesn't rush the process,
because you trusts the Builder.*

*May you rest without guilt.
Set boundaries without explaining.
Release without regret.
Forgive without reopening wounds.
And obey without needing applause.*

*May God strengthen you when you're tired,
cover you when you feel exposed,
and remind you again and again
that being "in the making" is not being behind.*

*You are not late.
You are not forgotten.
You are not disqualified.*

*You are becoming.
And God is faithful.* **Amen.**

www.ingramcontent.com/pod-product-compliance
Lightning Source LLC
LaVergne TN
LVHW091717070526
838199LV00050B/2431